TIME
FOR THE
TALK

The Ten Step Plan for Effective
Senior Caregiving Today

CLARICE W. DOWDLE

To —
My dear friends
Mimi, Bill
♡ Clarice

∞ INFINITY
PUBLISHING

Copyright © 2012 by Clarice W. Dowdle

ISBN 978-0-7414-7752-1 Paperback
ISBN 978-0-7414-7753-8 eBook
Library of Congress Control Number: 2012942555

Printed in the United States of America

Published July 2012

INFINITY PUBLISHING
1094 New DeHaven Street, Suite 100
West Conshohocken, PA 19428-2713
Toll-free (877) BUY BOOK
Local Phone (610) 941-9999
Fax (610) 941-9959
Info@buybooksontheweb.com
www.buybooksontheweb.com

DISCLAIMER

This book is based upon the personal experiences and perspectives of the author. Although the author has quite a lot of experience and insight into the subject of caregiving, she is not a medical professional, therapist, psychiatrist, or psychologist. She hopes that this book will contribute to a more significant understanding of the aging process, and will offer a new understanding of options available when caring for parents and loved ones.

For my parents, grandparents, in-laws, relatives, and inspiring seniors that have passed through my life, for my brother Fran and sisters, Jackie and Geri, who understand what playing on a team is all about, for all my amazing supportive friends, for Margot, Chuck, Lisa and Jeffrey, my God-sent editor, Ed, and for my very special daughter, Christina, who will one day be my caregiver. Like I have always said "when I grow old, just wheel me down to the beach with a lobster roll and I will be happy".

INTRODUCTION

Throughout most of my life I have been a caregiver in some form or another. I understand how the system works well, and how it doesn't. I have had many moments of joy but, unfortunately, more in tears. I am determined to make senior caregiving better for my generation, so that one day my daughter will have an easier time than I.

I want to open up the "treasure box" of aging and as deserved, make one's elder years meaningful, remembered, and filled with dignity. That is why writing this book for you is so important to me.

For over 40 years I have been somehow involved in experiencing the constant senior aging dilemmas. I can remember at a very early age going to visit my grandfather in a nursing home. Since it was pretty far away from where we lived, we could only visit a few times a month . . . a large white house on beautiful grounds . . . sounds lovely. But as you entered, not so lovely. Uniformed nurses cared for the elderly, some residents unable to speak or hear, or walk or even move . . . all lining the halls and darkened rooms. It was a sad state of existence. It was like a place you went to die. Somehow my grandfather "escaped" weekly, putting my mother in an utter panic. Knowing we would not be visiting again for some time, my mom would cry the whole way home after seeing grandpa. My first memories of senior care.

The first lesson, keep your loved ones close.

Years later, my grandmother was living independently in her own home until my dad found mice in her oven and unattended pots of boiling water on the stove. Grandma loved her home and her garden, and being so close to her church, but for safety reasons alone, she could not live by herself. She soon thereafter, kicking and screaming, was placed in a nursing home close to "our" house. My dad visited every day, and the rest of the family quite frequently. Although very challenging, we brought her to our home as much as possible for cookouts and holiday events.

Transporting someone in a heavy wheel chair back then was not easy, especially getting her up several outdoor stairs. When we would return to the "home," I vividly remember the aching sounds of patients and the horrific smell of urine from the moment you walked through the door. And the "help me" screams coming from some of the rooms. She lived there for over 10 years and died there at age 93. Even then, I thought there must be a better way to live and die.

Second lesson, listen to what she wants and needs, and accommodate those needs, even if it is more of a challenge for you.

My dad was an extremely talented musician; he could play all kinds of instruments from the piano to the violin, guitar, flute, and accordion. He would sometimes come sing and play music for my grandmother, which she enjoyed so very much. Soon, he realized that all her elderly companions also liked to hear him sing "their old songs," so he created a small business singing and playing the keyboard at nursing and assisted living homes for seniors in the Detroit area.

I would often go with my dad to hear him play his music. It was amazing to see the faces of such sad lifeless residents light up when the microphone would turn on. Some patients (if they could) would even get up and dance! He must have played over 500 times in some 25 years. I visited a lot of senior facilities during that time and hoped I would never have to live in one, no matter how great the music was. But the good news is that I have seen an incredible change over the years . . . much more attentive caregivers, nicer and cleaner environments, better food choices, personalized attention, and a full calendar of activities.

Third lesson, keep people busy and active, they will be happier.

My mom became ill in the late 1990s, needing home assistance, rehab, and, eventually in 2002, her life ended in a nursing home. At first, home caregivers were great for her, she felt they were attentive, she could confide in them . . . and they would listen, making this a generally positive experience. My dad disliked them because he felt it was an intrusion into their life — his life — and that he could handle her care on his own. Big Mistake. She had a few temporary stays in rehab where she was amongst a mixture of addicts and post surgery patients . . . not pleasant at all. She always just wanted to "go home." Was anyone listening? So, with limited capacity, understanding, and tolerance, my dad attempted to be her home caregiver, a hard job for anyone, let alone if you are not in the best of health yourself. That lasted until early one morning when a stranger walked into my dad's bedroom and said, "Your wife is lying on the front lawn screaming." Into the nursing home my mother went, drugged with morphine and an hour of hospice, consoled by an exhausted, disconnected husband of 50 years. She died a few days later at age 76. I am, although, grateful that, along with my brother and sisters, we could be at her bedside during her final days and hours.

I felt guilty because I lived far away and couldn't do more, I blamed my father for not doing a "good enough job", and I felt the situation could have been handled better. I did not know it had gotten so bad. My dad needed more help, my mom needed a "different kind" of assistance, and the communication channels had broken down. It was one of the worst times of my life. And when my mother closed her eyes for the last time, I literally jumped on top of her screaming! This was not possible. My mom could not have just died, she could not have left me, how could this have happened? This was not the way life was supposed to turn out. My dad was to die first, my mom was going to move to be near me in Atlanta. I was absolutely in total denial and shock. The shock waves continued for several years, facing the reality that she was really gone, gone forever.

Fourth lesson, get the care, support and help you need, don't be afraid to ask, and communicate with your family.

In the meantime, I had been hired by the Atria Assisted Living Company in Atlanta to handle all their PR and marketing efforts — the perfect client for me. Not only was I a marketing professional, but I had first hand knowledge of how senior living facilities were run, and what it was like to be a patient/resident. As part of my research with Atria, I visited a dozen or more assisted living homes in Atlanta and Maine, giving me a pretty good idea what the competition was like and what they each offered.

What a huge change had taken place in the industry in just a short time. These homes were lovely: beautifully carpeted and furnished, spacious rooms, lots of light, comfortable common area spaces, and elaborate dining rooms, not to mention the services offered. Hair salons, off-campus events, loads of activities and exercise programs, not to mention medical care and wonderful dining experiences in or out of you room. Some were even pet friendly!

The fifth lesson, figure out what is important to you and your loved one(s) do your homework, and you will find what you need.

Eventually, my own in-laws required some senior assistance. So we placed them in an Atria development just minutes from our home in Atlanta. Atria created a beautiful environment, provided constant care and attention along with activities to keep them busy (or not) from morning until night. They could even decorate their suite with their own furniture, paintings, and special belongings, making their environment more "like home."

I often brought my daughter over in the evening before bedtime in her pajamas to visit her grandparents, along with her dog, Cookie. Their eyes would brighten each time her sweet little face would enter their room. I even brought her Brownie troop over to make cookies. Their son, Chuck, would come by every day, sometimes even joining them for lunch. Other family members and friends would drop by just to say "hey." Their life was active, safe and secure. Unfortunately life is not forever, and they both died within a few months of each other after 65 years of marriage.

Lesson six, you can only do your best.

My dad had been living independently for about 10 years after my mom had died, although he had a tremendously long list of illnesses. My dad was determined to remain in his home in Michigan during this period, so all of my siblings got together and made a yearly visiting schedule to check on him. It is one thing to have daily talks on the phone but quite another to have a first-hand visit. We all went back and forth from

Denver, Dallas, Baltimore, and Atlanta to Grosse Pointe on a 6-week rotating schedule, as well as during numerous emergencies. We had learned from the past to constantly communicate with each other, to make a plan, and stay on top of our dad's medical needs and financial situation.

Finally, in January of 2011, after a severe back injury, he agreed to move to Atlanta where I could care for him. I placed him in a wonderful nursing home/rehab center, 15 minutes from me, and 5 minutes from the hospital. I had him transported by ambulance, and by the time he arrived, his room was decorated with his favorite artwork, plants, and flowers. I even brought his favorite juices and snacks and had an open closet built so he could enjoy looking at his collection of colorful shirts he so enjoyed. I had learned from my previous caregiving experiences that "making him feel at home" would be essential to his positive outlook and recovery. Although he wasn't at "his" home in Michigan, he felt "at home" in his special room. He went through extensive rehab and actually starting making great improvements, so much so that by April we were visiting almost every assisted living home in Atlanta for a "look see."

I was pleasantly surprised to see all the wonderful places available and what they all offered . . . one even had a movie theatre! We came for "lunch" visits and a tour. We enjoyed everything from homemade soups to shrimp scampi and red velvet cake . . . we ate our way through Atlanta. My dad loved great food, so finding a place right for him involved researching the daily menus. Since my dad was becoming more mobile, I ordered a transport wheel chair. That made my life a whole lot easier since I could easily lift it in and out of the trunk. I visited my dad every day. I brought him the paper, new shirts, and cookies, and sometimes one of his favorite home cooked meals. We played Scrabble and bingo, and went to all the special concerts, even Elvis night! I took him on all kinds of outings from a Braves game to the Atlanta Aquarium, to fun places for lunch and shopping. I took pictures of him wherever we went to forward to my brother and sisters, to keep them involved. We talked and talked and talked again.

My friends came, our dogs came . . . we all came and became part of the nursing home family. We got to be close with the amazing caregivers, and administration, and the residents, and especially the dietician and head chef, who would cater to my dad's every whim. But one day my dad said, "Am I going to be here for the rest of my life? Is this it?" And within a week we were moving to a beautiful assisted living home a few miles away. He had the ultimate "senior" bachelor pad . . . complete with a 52-inch TV and surround sound, and transfer poles to help him get up, as well as a lift lounge chair and bed. The perfect pad for an 87-year-old man. He was in his glory, meeting all kinds of new people, sharing stories, and even courting a lovely lady in the building. He was happy, enjoying the attention, loved his apartment, raved about the food, and had no worries because all was being taken care of.

No house worries, no fears of being alone, no concerns regarding meals or laundry or medicines. And even though he enjoyed his surroundings, our "outings" were very special to him, so I made a point to make those as frequent as possible. Unfortunately, a falling accident and a bout of pneumonia as well as heart failure all took their toll. He passed away in July of 2011. Since my brother and sisters and I were in such close contact we easily prepared his final resting plans. Everyone had a job to do, and we created a wonderful tribute to his memory. All of the lessons of the past do's and don'ts of caregiving became quite apparent . . .

finally, with my dad, all was honorable, peaceful and "just right". All of my previous experiences in caregiving presented themselves again, so I could be a better senior caregiver this time, and know, in the end, my dad's wishes were honored and that he knew he was deeply respected, cared for, and loved. Isn't that what we all want?

Lesson seven, no regrets.

TABLE OF CONTENTS

CHAPTER 1

Why are we here?

For some reason you have become the chosen one. From all of your brothers and sisters, relatives and friends, you are the one that has stepped up to the plate and said, "Yes, I will take care of you." Knowing full well you really don't know what you are getting yourself into, you agree to take on the task. You really don't know about the emotional commitment to your family member or parent(s) that is about to drive you into mental exhaustion. You have no idea about the endless phone calls, worry and visits to physically drive you to your knees. Let alone the mountain of financial and other paper-work that will seem to bury you. And that is on a good day, when nothing goes wrong.

My own journey with my grandparents, parents and in-laws was a hard one. I always felt things could have been handled an easier way, maybe a different way that made more sense. I was the one always asking "why?" Why were the results not back? Why has the doctor not come yet? Why has my mom not received her pain medication? Why, why, why. Oh, I am sure they loved to see me coming . . . "Here comes the daughter!" . . . darn right, HERE I COME! So, yes, you are now me!

Although I must tell you, I was one of the lucky ones. My brother and sisters came together to be the ultimate support team. No one can do this job alone, it does take a team effort.

1

And, in a perfect world all of your efforts will lead to a safer, healthier life for your loved one(s).

In the following chapters we are going to talk about everything I can think of to make your experience as a senior caregiver a better one. We are going to touch on every subject possible so just maybe you could do a better job than I did and earn your angel wings along the way!

CHAPTER 2

The Ten Steps

In the following chapters we will embrace what I call the "Ten Effective Steps to Caregiving." They start with the beginning of the discovery that your elderly loved one(s) may soon be needing some assistance to the end of your journey as a caregiver, with the loss of someone dear. Each step is a process. You have to start at the beginning and wander through each stage, through its ups and downs and twists and turns until it suddenly all stops.

Chapter 1 is really just a page of thoughts, it focuses on why we are here in the first place, what job we have to do, and where we are heading together.

Chapter 2 is where we are now . . . outlining The Ten Steps.

Chapter 3 is all about coming to terms with the situation you and your family members are now facing. It is about the reality of the situation, how to get organized, and about preparing for asking the hard questions in the foreseeable future. It is here that we create our own "Pre-Aging Agreement" for our loved one(s).

Chapter 4 is about the "Time for the Talk," the actual conversations that are desperately needed in order to fulfill our parents' ultimate wishes. It is also about gathering the information needed to caregive effectively.

Chapter 5 discusses options and resources that are available to your family member, whether it be moving into an assisted living facility or staying in a home environment. This chapter gives you checklists you will need to evaluate to determine what course of action is right for your parent(s). No one answer is right for everyone, which is why this chapter is so important.

Chapter 6 explores the legal issues facing seniors today. Documents from wills and probate to Powers of Attorney will be reviewed so that you are totally aware of the importance of having this legal paperwork in order.

Chapter 7 investigates the various benefits available to your loved one(s) . . . some at virtually no charge! It is amazing how knowing where to look and what to ask can go a long way in finding wonderful solutions to senior aging issues.

Chapter 8 reviews the medical care and medications your family member receives. This discussion can be intimidating at times, but it really needn't be. It is simply about gathering the most accurate information you will need to make the best possible medical decisions for your mom or dad, or loved one.

Chapter 9, our longest chapter, discusses the ongoing maintenance plan needed for your family member. From hygiene to exercise, socialization to nutrition, we look at the issues that can be forthcoming, stabilized, or prevented. We focus on warning signs and positive reinforcement. This chapter also prepares you for what to expect as your parent ages, hopefully limiting surprises and enhancing action.

Chapter 10 gives you the guidance to create a support team for yourself as well as your parent(s). From the local community to the national level, the help you need is there.

Chapter 11 highlights my favorite part of being a caregiver: embracing this time and assembling "A Treasure Box of

Memories." It is about slowing down and listening, remembering and making your final time together most meaningful.

Chapter 12 covers preparing for the inevitable, the dying and death of your beloved family member. It is difficult to lose someone you love, though we all know such loss is part of living. Taking the time to plan effectively and carry out the best decisions possible will lessen the pain of these final days.

Chapter 13 is our final goodbye.

CHAPTER 3 / STEP 1

Come to terms with your situation

The Time Is Now

If you find yourself wondering whether the time has come to be actively involved in the lives, activities, and decisions of your aging parents or loved ones, then that time has indeed arrived. In fact, it may be overdue.

All too often we postpone coming to terms with the aging and mortality of our parents until dad has a stroke or mom falls and breaks her hip, and the crisis calls for our immediate attention. Preparing and organizing for the inevitability of caregiving well in advance of any pressing need is essential for a successful outcome.

But our reluctance in the face of this prospect is natural enough. Few people are eager to contemplate their own senior years, let alone discuss the last years of life with their aging parents. So you wait for your parents or loved ones to approach the subject with you, and they wait for you to bring it up to them. It is ok actually it is essential – to discuss this topic, although it may be difficult. You have now been given permission to start the process. Both parents and caregivers need to know aging is a part of life, that life is about aging from the day you are born. The key is to make this discussion as comfortable as one can with the least amount of emotion possible.

You are far from alone in your predicament. A survey taken by the American Association for Retired Persons (AARP) found that fully 54 percent of Americans between the ages of 45 and 55 are caring for both growing children and aging parents. These people make up the so-called "sandwich generation," centrally positioned between a rising generation and a waning one. To get an idea of the task that lies before the sandwich generation, consider that, in 1950, the U.S. had 100 million citizens older than 60. By 2025, this number will grow by a factor of five, to 500 million.

Some members of the sandwich generation respond to the idea of parental caregiving by assuming that they now are reversing roles and becoming the parent of their own mother and father. Such is definitely not the case. Our parents will always be our parents, just as our sisters and brothers will remain our siblings. They are adults, as we are, and we owe them due respect, as we do any adult. Old age is not a return to childhood. *Our primary purpose in caregiving is to ensure that our parents exercise as much independence as possible for as long as they can.* To accomplish this goal, we must learn from our parents and loved ones what they wish for in their senior years, as well as the final days of their lives. We will desire such freedom and respect for ourselves when we arrive at that state in our own lives.

Signs of the Time

What signs can mark the onset of a parent's need for care? Consider just a few of these:

- Forgetfulness.
- Declining interest in activities.
- Lack of energy.

- Signs of depression – obsessive negativity, sadness, passivity, uncommunicativeness.
- A tendency toward withdrawal into isolation as abilities decline.

Physically, they may begin to have difficulties walking, and need to use a cane or walker. At a more subtle level, you may discover the electricity has been turned off because dad forgot to pay the bill. Mom may have problems driving her car, riding the brake with her left foot while controlling acceleration with her right. Activities of daily living — bathing and grooming, for instance, or cooking food — become problematic. Generally speaking, any noticeable deterioration in your parents' abilities to care for themselves should get your attention, particularly if such declines affect their day-to-day safety.

Responding to the Times

The question then arises: how do you respond?

Two keys are critical to your success:

- Your awareness of and sensitivity to the needs of others, beginning with your parents, but extending to fellow caregivers including siblings, friends, neighbors, and even professionals.
- Your ability to plan and organize a collective response in advance of its need.

In most cases, one family member, typically a female, becomes *the primary caregiver*. She may be the oldest child or, perhaps, the child geographically nearest the parents. The ten steps of this plan are addressed to that caregiver.

Parents will bring their own issues to the process, and you should not be surprised if longstanding problematic attitudes toward you resurface in these new circumstances.

Try to discuss matters early in the day, when older people are more rested and alert. If they change the subject whenever you raise the possibility of altering their routines, getting help, or moving, you may find it useful to begin some planning for your own later years. Your parents may respond more positively to the idea of addressing their own aging if they see you engaged in the same process. Or you might discuss plans of their contemporaries whom they respect, or relatives they are fond of who are making life-changing decisions. These ideas may stimulate interest on their part.

How does your aging parent or loved one wish to spend her senior years and last days? You might begin by exploring a little family history: ask her how she dealt with her own parents in their declining years. Her actions then may provide clues to what you might do now. Where does she wish to live while she is relatively healthy or if a crisis occurs? How does she feel about nursing homes, about senior communities and assisted living facilities? Would she want live-in help or to move in with you and your family?

The answers to such questions will evolve and change with the passage of time, which will take its slow but steady toll on your loved one's prospects and abilities. The point is to get, at the outset, an idea of what she wants in her declining years. This general idea will encompass everything from living situations to health care matters to end-of-life issues and decisions.

Examine your loved one's habits, for they dictate and determine her needs, and you should let them guide caregiving selection. If Mom gets up at 6:00 every morning and eats a queen-sized breakfast, you will have to find caregivers – or *be* the caregiver – who can satisfy this need. When does she bathe and groom herself for the new day? Can she accomplish these activities by herself, or will she need assistance? How does she prefer the household chores to be done? Is she a stickler for perfection, for doing everything just so, or is she easy going and readily pleased? Does she watch television into the early morning and rise at noon? Whatever the case, your selection of caregivers will have to conform to your loved one's habitual lifestyle.

You might expect resistance as you initiate the caregiving project, and this resistance may come not only from your aged parents or loved one, but also from siblings and other members of your family. None of us wants to grow burdensome in old age, and the first response to the process is likely to be denial. Denial is a first step in the process of grieving, and natural to all of us. Allow your parents to experience their own aging at their own pace. Barring the onset of dementia, acceptance of reality will come. Recognize that you, too, are grieving the passing of the parent(s) you have known all your life.

Dealing with Siblings

Siblings also may offer resistance to the changes accompanying the onset of old age, and winning them over to your side of the caregiving process can be a very real challenge. Ideally, you will collaborate with your siblings on a caregiving plan that assigns responsibility equally among family members.

Like your parents or loved ones, your brothers and sisters may slip back into old roles in response to your requests for help. Generally speaking, any relationship that has been difficult in the past will remain difficult in the new present. Expect to encounter resistance and you will not be blindsided when you confront it. Be willing to look at matters from someone else's point of view, and to allow other caregivers to respond to various needs and situations in their own ways. *Above all, listen.* If you address the needs and concerns of others, they will be that much more likely to respond positively to your own.

Problems grow smaller when we share them with other people, so try to involve your siblings as early as possible in the caregiving process. Remember that they also have needs, wishes, and conflicts concerning your parents, and they probably want to help if they can. Excluding others at the outset may result in a lack of such help in the future.

Always be honest, as well as tactful, when dealing with others involved in the caregiving process. Calmly share your own position, experience, and concerns, and avoid commenting on the degree of assistance you receive from others. Ask for help rather than assigning tasks. Watch for any tendencies you may have toward perfectionism. Another sibling might help out in a way different from yours, but refrain from criticizing anyone's performance. Above all, express your thanks whenever someone else pitches in.

Finally, be prepared to accept *no* as an answer. Some people you approach may simply refuse to participate. Other siblings' relationships with your parents may be too complicated and painful to allow them to function effectively as caregivers. Or they may simply be too busy with their own lives, families, and careers. Be prepared to accept and try to understand such rejection. Do not take it personally – it is usually not about you.

A Pre-Aging Agreement

Organization is key to the caregiving process. You cannot be too organized. You will need to organize information – your parents' or loved ones' vital data, as well as all sorts of paperwork concerning insurance, medical benefits, and legal documents, such as wills and powers of attorney. You will learn by trial and error as the process moves forward, and you will come to know your aged parent or loved one more intimately than you ever dreamed possible.

The need for such organization should encourage you to undertake the caregiving planning before circumstances force it upon you. One option you may wish to consider is what I call a *Pre-Aging Agreement* between your loved one(s) and the rest of the family. This document can initiate the dialogue necessary to successful caregiving of the aged. It can pose vital questions of your loved one's care at the end of her life while these concerns are still largely theoretical and may be considered rationally, free from the stress and strain of crisis. The Pre-Aging Agreement is not a legal document, but is a tool to foster discussion and understanding on the part of all family members concerned. It is also a means to begin gathering the information, such as data regarding Social Security benefits, health insurance requirements, and more, that will play an important role in the caregiving process. At the end of this chapter I provide a sample Pre-Aging Agreement, created specifically for this purpose.

The Inevitable

Along with our parents, we must come to grips with the inevitable outcome of our caregiving. Aging is a gradual but ongoing process of loss, where every day something is taken away, all leading to the ultimate loss of life itself. Aging is the natural complement to childbirth and -rearing, where every day something is added. The poignancy of this final stage of life will often move us and can sustain us in our caregiving.

Caregivers do run the risk of strong unpleasant emotions, including guilt, anger, and depression. About half of the respondents to the AARP survey felt they were not doing enough to help their parents; and this feeling bothered caregivers regardless of what they were actually doing. Asian-

Americans, for instance, were the most active of caregivers but also expressed the most guilt — 72 percent of those surveyed reported struggling with such feelings.

Anger forms a pitfall for caregivers as well, often in response to someone's refusal to cooperate — either an aged parent or someone assisting you with their care.

Most caregivers find that such discomforting emotions can arise repeatedly, like a nagging cold that won't quite go away, and a positive response can go a long way toward overcoming them. Instead of dwelling on guilt for what you are not doing, take an honest inventory of the things that you are doing. Chances are good that you are doing more than you think. In place of anger at someone else's failure to cooperate, examine the range of responses available to you. If someone else is unwilling to give, think of what you can you give.

Depression, a clinical phenomenon, is a risk factor as well, for both caregivers and their charges. Unrelenting and unreasonable self-criticism, profound and lasting sadness, loss of appetite, and insomnia are among the symptoms of clinical depression. If you find yourself confronting any or all of these symptoms, seek your own physician's guidance. Depression is not simply self-pity or a failing of character, but a medically treatable physical and mental condition. The stress of caregiving, between spouses and among siblings, can be difficult, and it plays a role in the onset of depression.

On the other hand, there are joys to be savored in your new role as caregiver. Much gratification may be derived from the knowledge that you are setting an example for the rising generation, those who will one day stand in your place. Additionally, a solid majority of respondents to the AARP survey (72 percent) said that caregiving had brought their families closer together. Increased intimacy with your parents and children, as well as with siblings and others on whom you come to rely, will mean much to you when the time for caregiving is over.

Sample Pre-Aging Agreement

<u>Wishes/Issues</u>

What are the most important wishes/issues facing your loved one(s) today and in the foreseeable future? The intent of this plan is to provide a basic template to best ensure happiness, security, safety, and peace of mind for your parent(s), family member(s), or loved one(s).

<u>Living Situation</u>

Evaluate current living situation
Potential future options
Drastic situation/change

<u>Support Team</u>

Primary caregiver
Support caregivers
Family members
Friends / Neighbors
Community
Church
Other organizations/clubs
Maintenance help, e.g. landscaping, cook, and housekeeper
Pet care
Life alert/emergency response
Include contact names, telephone numbers e-mail addresses, and permanent addresses

<u>Medical Assessment</u>

List of Physicians and Dentists
Physical therapist
Current medications and vitamins – list including name, dosage, reactions, and reason for taking

Allergies/other issues, e.g. implant devices

Prescriptions – pharmacy, cost, and applicable insurance/co-payments

Evaluate smoking/drinking habits

HIPAA rules

Include contact names, telephone numbers e-mail addresses, and permanent addresses

<u>Legal Documents</u>

Birth information/date(s) – exact legal name(s)

Social Security number(s)

Bank accounts – CDs, stocks, bonds

Investments

Trusts

IRA and 401k

Life insurance

Other insurance policies

Real estate

Mortgage and property taxes

Identification – birth certificate, Social Security card, passport, driver's licenses

Credit card information

Will – Living will, advanced directives, power of attorney, medical power of attorney

Marriage documents

Divorce documents

Safety deposit box – locations, keys, combinations

Citizenship papers

Business contracts

Legal agreements/documents

Property deeds

Titles

Location of tax returns – federal and state

Financial Review

Finances
Insurance
Medicare/Medicaid
Veteran's benefits
Pension
Social Security
Disability insurance
Property
Other income
Debts
Evaluate budget situation

Death and Dying

Life support
DNR (Do Not Resuscitate) orders
Organ donations
Final plans – burial and cremation
Final resting place, plans, and wishes
Financial arrangements

Review and Implement

TBD

CHAPTER 4 / STEP 2

Begin a dialogue with your parents and family –
It's Time for the Talk

An Ongoing Conversation

The list of people with whom you will need to confer regarding your parents' care may seem endless: siblings and other relatives, physicians, attorneys, clergymen, pharmacists, nurses, social workers, accountants, insurance companies, and more. But the most important dialogue will be the ongoing one between you and your parent(s) or loved ones themselves.

Barring mental incompetence, which will be addressed later in this book, your parent has the final word on her care and the limitations that she will accept. Such are his/her rights, and they include the right to be uncooperative, but that does not mean that they can take risks with their own health and safety. That is where you come in.

Imagination, and the empathy enabled by imagination, are your keys to responding to such situations. You will need, again and again, to put yourself in your parents' place and look at the world from their perspective. You will also have to honestly examine your own motives on occasion. Do you want mom to move into your guest bedroom because it is the best thing for her or because it is more convenient for you? If the latter, then the move may spell trouble in the longer run.

The management of her own life is of utmost importance to mom, and nothing involving her care should be done without her consent unless it is absolutely deemed necessary.

As we grow older, we lose our independence, one day at a time, and gradually surrender control over more and more areas of our lives. The process threatens our sense of self, an understanding of our identities built up over the course of our lives. This sense of who we are is very near the core of all human experience, and in old age we gradually surrender this concept in exchange for an unknown. As caregivers, we cannot be too conscious or too caring of what such a loss means.

Many older adults, for example, experience an embarrassing loss of bowel and bladder control, and our response to this situation reveals much about our capacity for empathy. Our parents must accept the realities of old age, and one of our tasks, as caregivers, is to gently assist them in this coming-to-terms with their life changes. Your father may be extremely reluctant to share his incontinence problem with a stranger at the local pharmacy. Although you can possibly step into his shoes and discuss it with him, and with his doctor, trying to find the best way to respond to this awkward but quite common situation. As a caregiver, you need to be willing to take on these issues such as shopping for adult diapers in order to assist your loved one(s) in responding to his changing needs. Once the initial learning experience is past, he may feel comfortable dealing with the matter himself, but not at first. No one likes to be alone with a problem, especially one of a highly personal and intimate nature.

Old age is like swimming into the ocean. You don't know what lies beneath, or if the water will be too cold or if it is deep or shallow or even if the seas will be calm or rough. It's your job as a caregiver to be the life vest for your loved one(s) – always there keeping them safe and afloat.

Ask your parents about their reality – their wishes, habits, preferences, desires, and dreams – and attend carefully to what they say. What is important to them? Living in their own home? Involvement in religious services? Driving their own car? Cooking their own meals? Visits with friends? Dining out or going to the movies? Living in Michigan or some other region of the country? Living closer to their children? Attending local events? Continuing a special club membership? The answers to such questions reveal your parents' perception of the changing limits of their lives, their understanding of the world in which they live. If we expect our parents to accept us as caregivers, we must first acknowledge the reality of their perspective on their own lives.

Finances

Matters involving money will almost certainly need to be addressed delicately. The generation that came of age during the Great Depression has a vastly different perception of financial affairs than do Baby Boomers. Money is a symbol of our independence and personal success, a highly personal part of life. Your desire to learn the details of your parents financial situation may threaten their idea of themselves as functional adults who can take care of themselves. Remember, no matter what happens, they will always look at you as their child, and that they changed your diapers! Their desire for privacy in financial matters must be carefully balanced with the reality that their care comes with a price tag.

If your loved ones have mismanaged their money, they probably will not want you to know it. They may be economizing by cutting down the heat or skimping on groceries. If they have been highly successful they may not want you to know that either, for fear they may feel you are caring for them "only for the money."

You might begin the discussion by speaking to them of your own financial situation, and inquiring into their methods of money management. If they respond to this lead, slowly bring the discussion around to their own financial planning, the amount of insurance they carry, and the levels of savings and investments to be drawn on for long-term care in their elder years. Take things slowly and easily, and, as they grow comfortable with the discussion, lead them to consider the facts of their situation, and to begin to formulate a considered and careful response to the financial realities of their aging.

You may want to discuss your parents' financial situation in the context of the Pre-Aging Agreement discussed in Chapter 3 / Step 1. You may approach it as a part of a general information gathering preparatory to the beginning of the caregiving process.

If your parents are adamant in refusing to share their financial lives with you, contact the local Area Agency on Aging, and ask to speak with a counselor, a neutral third party who can work with your loved ones in determining their needs, their resources, and their response. Or maybe this is where another sibling might do a better job than you. If so, pass on the torch to whomever will be most effective in dealing with this issue.

Of course, if your parent or loved one is making irresponsible decisions regarding his money because he is actually incompetent, you will have to take a more direct and forceful approach. Discuss the situation with his doctor and, if necessary, take steps to obtain a guardianship over him. At this time it is also a very good idea to pay close attention to your parent's friends and acquaintances. Any brand new person entering your mom or dad's life may certainly be well-intended. On the other hand, they may have another agenda in mind.

Issues of Control and Independence

Close on the heels of money matters come issues of personal control. Giving up the use of the car, and with it a large measure of their freedom and independence, is a major turning point in the aging process of most people. We tend to discount, if not deny, any impairment of our control over our own locomotion. Both AARP and the American Automobile Association (AAA) offer courses on driving in our later years. Your state division of motor vehicles may also offer assistance in the transportation needs of the elderly, particularly with regard to safety issues.

Alternatives to driving oneself include community services such as van runs offered by senior centers; public transit such as taxis, busses, and trains; and medical transport services. Often, such services offer a discount for seniors. Neighbors may be willing to pitch in from time to time and take mom to have her hair done or go grocery shopping. You also might consider hiring an eager college student to drive "Miss Daisy" on her rounds. Be sure to verify references and inquire into the background of any such hires. You may be able to arrange for your parents' transportation on an on-call basis. Keeping the "family car" in the garage or driveway may also be a good idea, it symbolizes not closing the door on driving entirely, just suspending it. It is just about "for now."

Home delivery is an alternative to shopping trips for groceries, meals, and prescription medicines. Usually such services charge a nominal fee, and often orders may be placed online.

Meals on Wheels is probably the most famous organization dedicated to providing nutritious food to seniors free of charge. The national Meals On Wheels Association (www.mowaa.org) represents local community-based senior nutrition programs in all the 50 states, as well as in the U.S. Territories. There are some 5,000 local senior nutrition programs in the United States, providing well over one million meals to seniors each day. Some programs serve meals at places like senior centers, while others deliver meals directly to homebound seniors. Many programs provide both services.

Another good option is available at Golden Cuisine (goldencuisine.com), which offers a complete line of ready-to-heat frozen entrees and shelf-stable meals specifically tailored to the nutritional needs of seniors. Affordability is a feature, as is ease of preparation and free delivery. Each meal comes packed in a rigid tray, safe for use in the oven and easy to handle, and with comprehensive cooking instructions. The range of items is extensive, including such meals as chicken broccoli Alfredo, turkey tetrazzini, spaghetti and meatballs, pot roast, and boneless pork patties. Multiple-package meals may be ordered in quantities of two, five, seven, and ten packs. Breakfast packs are also available, and shelf-stable meals such as rotini and meatballs, sweet-and-sour chicken, and orange beef are also available in multiple-package orders. A complete product list is available online at goldencuisine.com/products.asp.

On the other hand, if your parents are up to the effort, scheduled weekly or biweekly shopping trips will get them out of the house and into a bit of the life of the world. My own father used to joke that he had gone to the grocery store and come home with green bananas – a sure sign that he was going to stick around for a little while longer, waiting for them to ripen. He was incredibly fond of grocery-store trips. He enjoyed riding down the aisles in his electronic scooter, looking at all the new products offered, as well as meeting new people and visiting with his "regulars" at the checkout counters.

"Urban Villages" are also sprouting up from one end of the country to the other. The "village" program is really beginning to catch on, predominantly in New England and California. The organizations are comprised of as many as 150 or more volunteers who are available to help with senior needs. Everything from assistance with home repairs to driving to paperwork preparation is all available by making one call to their localized center. A yearly fee is usually attached for all services provided within this volunteer network. This is a great idea and a good concept; for more information, check your local city-wide directories.

Keeping Tabs and Keeping in Touch

Communication is a major part of every person's social life. Your loved ones have no substitute for personal visits from you, your siblings, and friends, but everyday communication can be enhanced by the use of cell phones and conference calls, and online resources such as family blogs, LISTSERVs and other automated emailing lists, and email. Of course, nothing can take the place of the old-fashioned letter from one person to another. Cards also are fun to receive in the mail. Since our parents did not grow up in the electronic age, mail has always been important to them, so using that method of communication is quite valuable. Do not overlook Skype, the voice-over-internet protocol service that enables communication by voice, video, and instant messages.

A means of contact with the outside world is critical in any medical emergencies. Life-alert pendants and bracelets are an alternative to cell phones. Usually available for a one-time setup charge and a monthly fee, these devices can alert a central response system to any problems your parents may encounter. But your charges must be willing to maintain and use such tools, which can do no good lying on the bedside table.

Many police departments offer senior watch programs, in which an elderly citizen checks in with the service on a daily basis. Special arrangements can be made for vacations and other absences from the home. Such a service is particularly helpful when the caregiver lives at some distance. You will also want to review your loved one's situation with an eye to personal safety, and take steps to install smoke and other alarms as needed.

At a minimum, ask neighbors to be your eyes and ears, simply taking everyday notice of your loved ones and their home. Be sure to thank them occasionally with a gift of some sort, or even financial remuneration, if appropriate.

Your parents will almost certainly have their own expectations and concerns about their senior years. Listen to their reality – their reasons for what they want, where they want to be, what they want to do, and how they want to live in their later lives. You may not understand the reasons why they want to live in Iowa but that is ok – it is what they want and it is their life to live.

Living Arrangements

As your loved ones age and become less independent, issues of place may need to be discussed. Should your loved one move closer to you or to another sibling? Consider this idea carefully. The move should be made not for the convenience of the caregiver, you, but in the best interests of your loved one. How will he fare once he is removed from his customary surroundings? Will he be able to see and to communicate with his friends and other family members? And will you be able to provide him with all the support, time, and care he will need in a new environment?

Moving closer to you makes sense if your loved one is unable to get around on her own, or if she has outlived all of her friends. If she needs to enter a nursing home, proximity to you will be of real significance.

Organization Begins with Information

Discussions of the Pre-Aging Agreement provide a context for exploring your loved ones' needs and wishes. Start gathering information on the following areas of their lives:

- Bank accounts, both checking and savings, as well as CDs, stocks and bonds, IRA and 401(k) accounts, and mutual funds, along with account numbers and the names of the financial institutions with which they do business. Do not neglect any security codes, or PINs, associated with these accounts.
- Life insurance policies.
- Homeowner's or renter's insurance policies.
- All information concerning real estate, including mortgages and property taxes.
- All forms of identification: Social Security numbers, passports, driver's licenses, and so on.
- Credit card account information, with photocopies of the cards, both front and back.
- Information regarding plans and requests for their funerals and burial, including any prepaid plans and mortuary arrangements.
- Contact information for health care providers – doctors, dentists, pharmacies, and so.

- Contact information on their neighbors and friends.
- Titles for all cars, boats, and any other vehicles.
- Locations of lock boxes and safe deposit boxes, with keys and combinations.
- Their complete medical history, together with a list of currently prescribed medicines.
- Living wills, advance directives, and a medical power of attorney.
- Any religious organizations with which they are affiliated.
- Certificates of birth, marriage, divorce, citizenship.
- Veterans papers.
- All business contracts, rental agreements, deeds to properties.
- Copies of all tax returns, both federal and state, for the preceding five years.
- A list of all debts.

If your loved one(s) have not addressed these areas yet, now is the time.

End-of-Life Issues

Of paramount importance is the question of what sort of medical measures your loved one wants as the end nears. Would he want to be resuscitated if his heart stopped or placed on life support should his faculties fail? Short of such heroic efforts, what *does* he want? Your parents' doctors may also be consulted regarding these decisions.

If aggressive measures are not to be taken in preserving your parent's life, reconcile yourself to the reality that you will have to say *no* if and when these options are presented.

This response is easier to imagine than to give. The caregiver who declines extraordinary efforts must be sure that her response is the honest expression of her parent's will.

In matters of diagnosis and prognosis, nothing substitutes for the truth. Actions prompted by the desire to preserve vain hopes will likely result in more suffering than relief, for your parent(s) and for you. As Henry David Thoreau says in *Walden*, "be it life or death, we crave only reality." Caregivers and those they love can begin today to accept the inevitable.

Meetings and More Meetings

Meet with your parents or loved ones in a one-on-one setting, and review all the matters discussed thus far. Then gather your family for a meeting on your parents' care, including, if possible, all siblings. Third parties, particularly physicians and clergymen, may also be consulted. The meeting may occur at a holiday gathering of the family or may be scheduled in a more formal manner.

Items to be considered at your initial meeting range from physician services and medication use to the timely payment of bills. On each issue, the point of departure will be the thoughts, wishes, and feelings of your parent(s) or loved ones.

You may want to employ an outsider to moderate the discussion if you think there may be conflicts, thus assuring all concerned of a measure of impartiality and evenhandedness in the conduct of the meeting. A moderator can see to it that all participants receive the time they need to speak and share their concerns and opinions. Doctors, clergy, respected family friends, and social workers are all possibilities.

You can find these human resources in your community by using the Web-based eldercare locator at www.eldercare.org, or by calling 1-800-677-1116. This service is maintained by the

National Association of Area Agencies on Aging, which may be accessed at www.n4a.org.

Organization will be essential to the success of any such meetings, and to the whole project of caregiving. In all likelihood, family meetings of some sort will become a regular feature of your family life. At a minimum, some sort of monthly conference call can be made to keep everyone up-to-date and on the same page. Use of a written agenda for such meetings and discussions is a good idea. The agenda could be circulated among the participants before the meeting actually occurs, to ensure the completeness of the discussion.

You cannot be too organized, especially in the areas of vital information concerning your parent's or loved ones' stability and long-term happiness.

CHAPTER 5 / STEP 3

Review your options and resources

The Living Arrangement

What sort of living situation best suits the needs of your aging parent or loved one? The answer will depend primarily on the degree of help he or she needs on a daily basis, but other factors, such as safety issues, the presence of other people in the household, and practical matters such as cooking, laundry, and mobility also figure into the solution.

Perhaps your loved one, though needing your attention as a caregiver, can largely take care of herself and continue to live in her own home. Note that physical rehabilitation therapy may play a role in making this possible. What changes will need to occur to make this possible?

Safe and Sound

Safety is the Number 1 issue. Among the elderly, accidents are the sixth leading cause of death, and your parent's home should be thoroughly evaluated with safety in mind.

Scatter rugs form a real trip hazard. If your parent uses them cosmetically, to cover stains, get rid of them. If they serve a real purpose, such as covering a slippery part of the floor, use rugs with nonskid backings and fasten them to the floor with carpet tacks. If at all possible, replace them all with new carpet or room-size area rugs.

Ideally, your parent's home will occupy only one level. If stairs are present, all should be identical in height, width, and depth, with handrails that run the full length of the flight. Stair edges may be marked with brightly colored, eye-catching tape. Replace stairwell carpeting with nonskid treads.

Clutter – or, depending on your point of view, treasures -- can also be problematic, not only as trip hazards but as fire risks. Some elderly people are given to hoarding all sorts of things, old newspapers and magazines among them. They may become seriously attached to these items and actively resist their removal. But these items are fire hazards and may also obstruct movement in the house. Some negotiated compromises will be necessary. You might ask your fire department to send a representative to the house to discuss the hazards with your parent or loved one. At the worst extreme, call Adult Protective Services anonymously and let the government play the villain's role in disposing of all the disorder.

Unnecessary furniture should be moved to rooms that are not in use. If your parent or loved one is using the furniture as a handhold to navigate her way through the house, insist that she employ a cane or walker instead.

Safeguarding against Falls

Falls in the bathroom can be literally deadly. Grab bars should be installed at critical points such as the edge of the bathtub, beside the sink, and near the toilet and the door. Raised toilet seats with attached bars are a good solution for bathroom visits. Bathtub chairs are an option to reduce the risks of showering. The shower curtain rod should be mounted to the wall with screws, not held in place by tension, to provide a real handhold in the event of slips. Bath mats should have nonskid backings. Bars of soap should be replaced by bottles of the liquid kind. Ideally, a liquid soap dispenser should be installed by the sink to spare your parent the risks of fumbling for soapy bars.

Ensure that the house is well and evenly lit, with light switches that are easy to see and use. Place a light on the bedside table so that your parent does not have to navigate in darkness to get to the bathroom during the night. Motion-detector lighting is most desirable. Night lights may also be placed in hallways, stairs, and kitchens.

Seniors sometimes need supplies of oxygen, which come with the attendant hazards of tanks and yards of tubing, which can be hazardous to the spouse as well as the patient. Fasten tubing to the floor with the same brightly colored, eye-catching tape you used to mark stair edges. Also, monitor the tanks carefully. If the mechanisms do not function properly, they are in danger of failing.

Sometimes looking at your parent's living situation with a "new pair of glasses" may help you realize how simple changes can create a new, more suitable and safe environment. For instance, turning the first-floor dining room that seats twelve into a first-floor master bedroom makes a lot of sense, since it is highly unlikely that large dinner parties will continue to occur. Also, adding an outside ramp instead of stairs would be a much safer way to enter the home. This is the time to think "outside the box" to create the most desirable living situation possible. It is amazing how creative we can all be once we open our minds wide to positive and productive change.

Smoke alarms are a necessity in anyone's home. Locate one just outside the kitchen – where it won't go off if your loved one singes the bacon – and one over every bedroom door.

In taking steps like these, you encourage independence and self-assurance on the part of your aging parent or loved one. Remember that, all things being equal, the more we do for ourselves, the better we feel about ourselves.

Moving in with You?

Of course, should your parent leave her home and move in with you, in a guest room or addition to the house, you will need to install all these safety features there as well. Other issues will arise in this situation, such as the presence you may have in the home and increases in cooking and laundry (seniors may need several changes of clothing each day).

Other factors to consider in contemplating your loved one's moving in with your family:

- Will everyone get along? A lot depends on your relationship with the parent or loved one. Is it characterized by mutual respect and accommodation, or is it rife with problems of long standing? Do your children delight your loved one or get on her nerves, and vice versa?
- Space considerations. Extended families get along better in larger homes.
- Does the home suit the needs of the loved one? For example, are the doors wide enough for a wheelchair?
- Can you satisfy your loved one's daily needs? How much care is required? And how much will be expected as time goes by?
- Are your lifestyles compatible?
- Do you have family and friends readily at hand to give you s break from your caregiving? Do your siblings support the move?

- Will any renovation of your home be necessary? If so, what will it cost?
- What sort of resistance might you expect, from your loved one and from other members of your family? Will your loved one see the move as a loss of independence? Will she feel that you are intruding into her private life, in matters such as finance and other personal matters? How do your siblings feel about the proposed new arrangement? Are they willing to take on any share of the caregiving? Planning the caregiving in concert with siblings can spare the whole family from great headaches.

There will, of course, be some intangible advantages in caring for your parent or loved one in your own home. Your children may grow closer to their grandmother or great aunt, and the experience of family life will be enriched by the presence of a third generation.

Alternative Lifestyles

Should your parent still be capable of independent living, *an apartment in a senior community* may be an option. Specifically designed for elderly tenants, these can range from lows of $300 a month, in subsidized housing available to people with low incomes, to as much as much as $1,500 a month or more. Find out what specific services are offered, and what provision is made for emergencies – is there a call button in each apartment, and does the facility have staff available to assist your parent or loved one at all hours of the day and night? What happens if your loved one falls ill? Also make sure that the apartments offer all the safety options discussed above.

Assisted Living

Assisted living facilities occupy a middle place between your parent's own home and a skilled nursing home. As the name implies, these facilities provide assistance, help, and support to seniors, in the form of housekeeping, meals, planned activities, and custodial care, while still allowing your parent substantial privacy and independence. Services can vary greatly from one facility to another, so find out exactly what is included for your parent(s) or loved one. For example:

- Is there custodial care – assistance with activities of daily living such as bathing and dressing?
- Is there any nursing care?
- What provisions are there for housekeeping? Will your loved one have to clean her own room?

Look for a facility that encourages independence and offers plenty of stimulation – outings and activities – while also offering your parent some privacy. Visit the prospective facilities on both formal tours and on unscheduled drop-ins during off-hours to see what the facility is like when it isn't necessarily putting its best face forward. Sample the meals and talk to residents and other families visiting, as well as the staff. Ask them about their opinions and concerns.

Note the level of functioning among the residents, looking for those who seem to be operating on a par with your parent. Do they seem to get along well with the staff? Do the everyday protocols of the facility encourage residents to remain as independent as possible? Review the male-to-female ratio, but above all examine the possibilities of "really living" there. Most importantly, does the facility feel comfortable to your loved one, and do you feel comfortable placing them there?

Assisted living costs can reach as much at $5,000 a month and more, depending on locations and offerings. The average nationally is about $2,500 a month, or $30,000 a year, but these figures do not cover all available options. Find out exactly what is included in the price and what is considered extra. Most private insurance will not cover the cost of assisted living, nor will Medicare. Long-term care insurance, however, covers room and board, and possibly a few extras.

Assisted living facilities can also go by a variety of names, such as personal care, sheltered care, and residential care, to name a few.

Note that to use all the facilities discussed thus far, your parent needs to be somewhat mobile. The following are some questions to consider in deciding on an assisted living facility.

Choosing the Right Assisted Living Home: A Checklist

- Will your loved one have a written plan for her care?
- Is your loved one's needs assessment an ongoing process? How often is it carried out?
- How does the facility respond when the needs of a resident change?
- Are there different levels of care available in designated building areas according to a loved one's condition?
- Is staff on duty 24 hours a day?
- Does the facility have special needs programs such as for Alzheimer's and dementia?
- At what frequency do the staff check on a resident's condition?
- How does the facility respond to verbally or physically abusive behavior on the residents' part?
- Does a nurse or physician do a regular check on the residents? What is the extent of available medical care?
- Does staff make medical appointments and arrange for the transportation of the residents?
- Does the facility's pharmacy review medicines and consult regarding them? Does it deliver? How do residents obtain their daily medications?
- Does staff oversee the administration of medicine, or do residents take responsibility for their own medications?
- What are the health care services available? Do they include physical therapy, social services, wound care, and hospice care?

- How does the facility respond to medical emergencies? Does the facility have an arrangement with a hospital or medical facility nearby?
- When will the facility contact the family? When will it contact your loved one's physician?
- Are housekeeping services, such as personal laundry and linens, included in the fee? Is there a convenient laundry facility on site?
- What sort of transportation does the facility provide? To doctors' offices? Shopping? Is such transportation available on short notice?
- Do you like the residence's appearance?
- Is the facility convenient to family and friends?
- How convenient is the facility for shopping and social outings in general?
- Is the facility conveniently served by public transportation?
- Is the atmosphere of the facility homelike and comfortable?
- Is the floor plan clear and easy to navigate?
- Does the facility's design accommodate wheelchairs and walkers?
- Is there an outside common area where residents can visit?
- Does the facility have elevators for those who cannot use stairways?
- Do handrails assist residents in walking?
- Are all floor coverings of nonskid materials?
- Is the facility clean, odor-free, and with an environment appropriate to the season?

- Does the facility have good lighting? Are there fire sprinklers? Are exits clearly marked? Is the emergency evacuation plan prominently displayed and easy to follow? Does staff conduct fire drills?
- How does staff respond to a resident who wanders?
- Is the new resident supplied with an emergency pendant?
- How many clients can the facility accommodate?
- Do the units have varying floor plans, or are they all the same?
- Does the facility offer private units, as well as double occupancies?
- What percentage of the units are currently occupied?
- If there is a waiting list, how long a wait is anticipated?
- Are rooms furnished, unfurnished, or both?
- Can your loved one decorate her own room? What is available in the way of storage?
- Can your loved one access 24-hour emergency assistance from her apartment?
- Are there private bathrooms? Do they feature handicapped accommodations?
- Does each unit have cable tv and a telephone? How are these amenities billed?
- Do kitchen units have refrigerators, sinks, and some provision for cooking?
- Can your loved one smoke in his unit? Are smoking areas designated in public areas?

- Does the facility proved three balanced meals each day, all through the week? Ask to see a menu for a typical week?
- Are menus planned and approved by a qualified dietitian? Will your loved one's weight be monitored?
- Can residents request special foods or a special diet?
- Does the facility have community dining areas?
- Are meals provided on a set schedule or will your loved one have some flexibility in the matter? What about the availability of snacks?
- How many meals does the fee cover? If your loved one falls sick, may he be served in his room?
- Can your loved one have guests dine with her? If so, is there an additional fee?
- Can the facility accommodate special events in a private dining room?
- Can your loved one residents dine in his apartment?
- What is the facility's alcohol policy?
- What recreational activities are available?
- Does the facility host an organized activities program? Is a schedule of activities posted regularly?
- Can family members or volunteers participate in or conduct programs within the facility?
- Does the facility schedule regular outings for the residents?
- Are supplies for social activities or hobbies, such as games, crafts, computers, and gardening, readily available to residents?

- Does the facility host regular religious services, or must arrangements be made for off-campus trips?
- What does the residence do to create a sense of community among the residents? What community activities are available?
- Are pets allowed?
- Is there a daily exercise program, with designated gym and rehab areas?
- Who is in charge of this program?
- Look around. Do the residents socialize? Do they seem to be comfortable?
- Will your loved one(s) get along with the other residents?
- Can you visit your loved one at any time, or are there restricted hours?
- How is the facility staffed? Are background checks required?
- Is there an ongoing training program for staff? What does it encompass?
- During your visit, is the administrator on hand to answer questions? Will you be comfortable with the administrator on a regular basis?
- What is the ratio of staff to residents?
- What is the length of a shift for staff?
- What is the staff turnover rate?
- Are staff courteous to clients and to each other?
- Do staff respond adequately to your questions?
- How does the staff deal with aggressive residents?
- Is the residence license or certification current?
- Is the administrator licensed or certified?

- Does the facility belong to any trade or professional associations?
- What is the reputation of the facility in the community? How long has it done business? What is its financial position?
- For a facility sponsored by a nonprofit organization and managed under contract with another firm, what conditions apply?
- Is there any mechanism for residents and family members to voice their views on the policies and management of the facility?
- Does the contract clearly describe health care, accommodations, personal care and supportive services, including all fees? What about admission and discharge provisions?
- Will your loved one manage his own finances? If not, who does?
- What is the schedule for payments?
- Do residents own their apartments or rent them? Is renters' insurance required to cover personal property?
- What is the history of increases in monthly fees?
- What are the costs for different levels of service?
- Can the facility accommodate skilled nursing care or physical therapy on a temporary basis?
- If your loved one must visit a hospital, will his room be held for him? Are you charged for this?
- When may an agreement be terminated? What are the policies regarding refunds and transfers?
- If your loved one is dissatisfied with any services, what recourse has she to appeals?

- What will happen if full payments can no longer be made?
- What government, private, or corporate programs exist to help with costs?
- Do you think the billing, payment, and credit policies are fair?

Nursing Homes

On the spectrum of senior care, *nursing homes* are the next step past assisted living facilities. These homes are also known as *skilled nursing facilities,* for that is the type of service they provide. They may also be referred to as SNFs ("sniffs"). Generally, a nursing home offers custodial care and skilled nursing care, on both a temporary or a long-term basis. Your parent will remain in such a facility as long as her care results in measurable gains, although some may call for ongoing skilled care, such as the need for ventilators and other mechanical means of life support.

Skilled care may be provided by a therapist (physical, occupational, or speech) or by a nurse. Your parent's care will be prescribed by a physician, and any licensed practical nurses (LPNs) employed will be supervised by a register nurse on staff. Most facilities have weekly on-site physician visitation.

Costs for SNFs can be as high at $70,000 a year and more. In Atlanta, the average cost is $5,400 a month. These costs are increasing, and are expected to continue to do so in the future. Such care is paid for only in part by Medicare and most private insurance adhering to Medicare guidelines.

Medicare requires that residence in a nursing home be preceded by a three-day hospital stay, with admission to the SNF occurring within the next 30 days. Medicare pays in full for your loved one's first 20 days, but requires a co-payment for the next 80 days. Beyond this 100-day period, Medicare pays nothing. Some of these deductibles may be covered by so-called Medigap insurance, purchased from private companies and designed to provide coverage where Medicare does not. Medicare pays only for medically prescribed nursing care and does not cover custodial care – the help with activities of daily living that is most needed by seniors.

The rules vary concerning Medicaid support for nursing home care, because the program is jointly operated by the federal and state governments. Medicaid covers most of the cost of a skilled nursing facility. In fact, Medicaid pays for nearly 50 percent of all the nursing home costs in the United States, so it is almost universally accepted by most facilities. Each facility, however, may set a limit on the number of Medicaid cases, or beds, it accepts. And of course, Medicaid is only available to people of low income and few assets.

Choosing a Nursing Home

The choice of a nursing home should be made with considerable care. Take the time necessary to examine all your options. Be sure to visit the your prospects' facilities unannounced and at random times, to ensure that the home lives up to your expectations.

Nursing homes are evaluated and rated according to their potential for harm to residents and for violations of state and Medicare regulations. Color-coded ratings range from a low of "actually experienced harm" on the part of residents to a high of "no violations of regulations." You may view these ratings at http://memberofthefamily.net, and you will want to review these rankings before scheduling actual visits.

You should also consider the Medicare Five-Star Quality Rating System, which includes inspection results, nursing home staff data, quality measures, and fire safety inspection results. This system was created to help families compare nursing homes and easily identify questions to ask when beginning the search process. You may find it on the Web at www.medicare.gov/NHCompare.

Other factors in your decision include:

- Proximity of the home to family and friends of your loved one.

- Certification by the federal government (a criterion for Medicare and Medicaid coverage).
- Maintenance and cleanliness – a nursing home should not have a musty, sour smell to it.
- Staffing levels of at least 1:5, direct-care staff to residents.
- Staff turnover.
- Active residents, encouraged to maintain as much independence as possible and engaged in stimulating activities that get them up and around.
- Communication with and access to directors and floor managers.
- Space availability – is there a waiting list and, if so, how long is it?
- Availability of medical and nursing care.

Above all, be sure that your loved one feels at home and comfortable in her new surroundings. The living space should easily accommodate familiar personal items and keepsakes without worry of theft. The staff should be knowledgeable and friendly. The food should be tasty and served at the proper temperature, with appropriate presentation. Residents should seem to be relatively happy with their situation. *Ask your loved one's opinion* of the facilities available, allowing her to participate in the decision.

Our guide to choosing the right nursing home for your loved one(s) follows.

Choosing the Right Nursing Home: A Checklist

- Is the nursing home Medicare-certified?
- Is the nursing home Medicaid-certified?
- Does the nursing home have the level of care we need?
- Does the nursing home have a bed available?
- Does the nursing home offer specialized services, such as a special unit for care for a resident with dementia, ventilator care, or rehabilitation services?
- Is the nursing home located close enough for friends and family to visit?
- Are the residents clean, well groomed, and appropriately dressed for the season or time of day?
- Is the nursing home free from overwhelming unpleasant odors?
- Does the nursing home appear clean and well kept?
- Is the temperature in the nursing home comfortable for residents?
- Does the nursing home have good lighting?
- Are the noise levels in the dining room and other common areas comfortable?
- Is smoking allowed? If so, is it restricted to certain areas of the nursing home?
- Are the furnishings sturdy, yet comfortable and attractive?
- Does the relationship between the staff and residents appear to be warm, polite, and respectful?
- Does the staff wear name tags?

- Does the staff knock on the door before entering a resident's room? Do they refer to residents by name?
- Does the nursing home offer a training and continuing education program for all staff?
- Does the nursing home check to make sure they don't hire staff members who have been found guilty of abuse, neglect or mistreatment of residents; or have a finding of abuse, neglect, or mistreatment of residents in the state nurse aid registry?
- Is there a licensed nursing staff 24 hours a day, including a Registered Nurse (RN) present at least 8 hours per day, 7 days a week?
- Will a team of nurses and Certified Nursing Assistants (CNAs) work with my loved one to meet her needs?
- Do CNAs help plan the care of residents?
- Is there a person on staff that will be assigned to meet my social service needs?
- If I have a medical need, will the staff contact my doctor for me?
- Has there been a turnover in administration staff, such as the administrator or director of nurses, in the past year?
- Can residents have personal belongings and furniture in their rooms?
- Does each resident have storage space (closet and drawers) in his or her room?
- Does each resident have a window in his or her bedroom?

- Do residents have access to a personal phone and television?
- Do residents have a choice of roommates?
- Are there policies and procedures to protect residents' possessions, including lockable cabinets and closets?
- Are exits clearly marked?
- Are there quiet areas where residents can visit with friends and family?
- Does the nursing home have smoke detectors and sprinklers?
- Are all common areas, resident rooms, and doorways designed for wheelchair use?
- Are handrails and grab bars appropriately placed in the hallways and bathrooms?
- Do residents have a choice of food items at each meal? (Ask if your favorite foods are served.)
- Can the nursing home provide for special dietary needs (like low-salt or no-sugar-added diets)?
- Are nutritious snacks available upon request?
- Does the staff help residents eat and drink at mealtimes if help is needed?
- Can residents, including those who are unable to leave their rooms, choose to take part in a variety of activities?
- Do residents have a role in planning or choosing activities that are available?
- Does the nursing home have outdoor areas for resident use? Is the staff available to help residents go outside?

- Does the nursing home have an active volunteer program?
- Does the nursing home have an emergency evacuation plan and hold regular fire drills (bed-bound residents included)?
- Do residents get preventive care, like a yearly flu shot, to help keep them healthy?
- Does the facility assist in arranging hearing screenings or vision tests?
- Can residents still see their personal doctors? Does the facility help in arranging transportation for this purpose?
- Does the nursing home have an arrangement with a nearby hospital for emergencies?
- Are care plan meetings held with residents and family members at times that are convenient and flexible whenever possible?
- Has the nursing home corrected all deficiencies (failure to meet one or more state or Federal requirements) on its last state inspection report?
- What improvements were made to the quality of life for residents in the last year?
- What are the plans for future improvements?
- How has the nursing home responded to recommendations for improvement?
- Who does the resident council report to?
- How does membership on the resident council work?
- Who sets the agendas for meetings?
- How are council decisions made (for example, by voting, consensus, or one person makes them)?

(This checklist may be downloaded in printable form from www.medicare.gov/NHCompare.)

Continuing Care Retirement Communities

Continuing care retirement communities (CCRCs) offer all the options to your aging loved one, providing for everything from independent living to skilled nursing care. Most admit only people who can function independently, but once accepted, your parent or loved one will receive whatever care he needs for the rest of his life. These communities feature apartments for the independent, as well as assisted living for those needing help with the activities of daily living, and skilled nursing home care for aging parents and loved ones reaching the end of life.

CCRCs charge a hefty entrance fee, which can range from $20,000 to more than half a million, and also carry monthly fees, from $500 to over $4,000. They offer three basic packages:

- All-inclusive contracts covering everything, including all nursing care.
- Modified coverage with a specific limit on the number of days per year of nursing care, with your loved one paying about 80 percent of the cost beyond the contracted amount.
- Fee-for-service contracts that cover the services of independent living and assisted living, but require your loved one to cover all nursing costs.

Factors to consider in evaluating a prospective CCRC include:

- The institution's financial stability.
- The refund policy.
- Certifications under Medicare.
- Costs excluded from monthly fees.
- Health insurance requirements.
- Number of nursing-home beds available.

Private Nursing and Health Care in the Home

The final options for your loved one to consider are *private nursing* and *medical care in the home*, both full- and part-time. Live-in and live-out shift care is available, at skill levels ranging from unlicensed companions to registered nurses.

Private-duty care agencies can facilitate the employment of such assistance. These agencies pay the staff's salary, taxes, Social Security, and worker's compensation. Many also check backgrounds and bond their employees, though these options should be verified in writing by the individual agency. Some agencies allow you to take on screened applicants on a trial basis, and then hire them directly, paying the agency a fee.

Private-care staff are usually trained in CPR and basic emergency response, and generally have a supervisor whom they can contact for any needed advice. Their work is governed by rules and regulations set by the federal, state, and local governments. Be sure to make a list of everything you need the staff to do, and to go over each item with the prospect. Professional restrictions may conflict with your job requirements. Certified nurses, for example, cannot dispense medication. Likewise, shopping trips and errands probably fall outside the range of prospective nursing staff.

Bending the Rules

Hiring privately, without the use of an agency, allows you to bend some of the rules. A caregiver directly hired by you may be instructed by you concerning the dispensing of medicines. However, you will also have to plan for the caregiver's own sick days, and you must assume the role of employer, paying her salary, plus all withholdings, Social Security, other taxes, and worker's compensation. You also will have total responsibility for any background check. On the other hand, hiring directly will allow you to get recommendations from your informal network of family, friends, co-workers, and other personal contacts. Churches and schools can also form a trustworthy source of information and a good referral base.

In-home care also requires the use of durable medical equipment (DME), such as walkers, canes, wheelchairs, and the bath fixtures discussed earlier. Some items, such a raised toilet seats and bedside commodes, must be purchased, and may be acquired from drug stores, catalogues, and at DME companies. Medicare covers 80 percent of DME costs, including hospital beds, wheelchairs, oxygen supplies, and walkers. Such big-ticket items may be purchased or rented.

There are a multitude of items that can be purchased to help your loved one(s) help themselves, such as grab bars, lift chairs, and wheelchairs, to name only a few. Investment in such items can be vital to a safer, more secure and comfortable existence. More information may be found on the Web at spinlife.com/Medicare and at activelivingnow.com.

And, always be sure to ask whether Medicare or your private insurance will pay for any of these items. You will be surprised at the number of items that can be provided to your loved one(s) at no cost at all.

CHAPTER 6 / STEP 4

Explore legal and financial issues

What legal and financial matters need attention in the case of your aging parent or loved one?

Wills and Other Legal Matters

Every adult who owns a home, or has other assets such as investments or a savings account, or who has children, should have a will. Simple wills can be drawn up by a lawyer for under $300. Do-it-yourself legal kits are also available for under $50. Look in the law section of your local bookstore. You may also create a will online for a modest fee, generally under $50. The legal publisher Nolo Press offers such a service at www.nolo.com/products/online-will-NNWILL.html. Your parents each should have a will of their own, because joint wills can lead to legal complications.

Wills may be updated with *codicils* and *letters of instruction*. A codicil amends the will without the necessity of rewriting the entire document. A letter of instruction generally expresses the decedent's wish with regard to a broad range of personal matters, ranging from the ownership of pets to the details of business affairs. Such a letter may also include instructions and suggestions to heirs concerning their inheritance and other affairs. These admonitions, however, fall into the category of advice — they are not legally binding.

A will is legally validated as genuine and authentic by a process known as *probate*, from the Latin *pr⊸bare*, meaning "to test and find good." This validation is done by a probate judge, and the process has the notorious connotation of being a protracted and expensive undertaking. Many states, however, have streamlined their probate processes, and it can often be completed by you alone, or with the assistance of a probate clerk.

If your parent or loved one leaves no will, her assets will be distributed by the probate court, a process that is time-consuming and could cost you a great deal of money. The hoops and hurdles of probate are a prime motive for creating a legally sound last will and testament.

Your loved one's will, along with any codicils and letters of instruction, should be kept in a safe place, and you should be able to access it with ease. Her safe deposit box is *not* a good place to keep it, for these often are sealed by a court when the parent or loved one dies.

Living Trusts, Revocable and Irrevocable

The will covers any and all assets of your parent's that will be placed in probate. The contents of a *trust*, on the other hand, are excluded from the will and do not pass through probate. This exemption also means that a trust is a more private affair than a will.

A trust is simply an alternative way to store assets. In a trust, property is held by one party for the benefit of another. Your parent or loved one, the *grantor*, places property of any kind "in trust" for his designated heirs. The properties are held on trust for the beneficiaries. Legally, that property belongs to the heirs and is not part of your loved one's estate. Thus, it is not subject to estate taxes.

A *testamentary trust* is one described in your loved one's will and established after her death. Such trusts are often employed to reduce estate taxes or to create a trust fund for a specific purpose, such as a child's education or some charitable purpose.

Your parent or loved one will probably be more concerned with two other types of trust, the *revocable living trust* and the *irrevocable living trust.* These are legal instruments, usually created by the grantor with the assistance of an attorney specializing in trusts and estate law. They are signed by the grantor and by the *trustee,* the person (or persons) who will administer and execute the trust after the grantor's death. Naturally, such a trust must be established while the grantor is still alive. The Latin name for this sort of trust is *inter vivos,* or "living" trust.

Revocable living trusts, as the name implies, may be changed by your parent or loved one at any time in her life. A revocable trust can even be undone altogether by the grantor. Revocable trusts, when crafted with care, may avoid the probate process altogether.

Irrevocable living trusts should be approached with great care, since, once created, they cannot be amended or revised until the terms of the trust have been implemented. The terms of a trust also appoint a trustee who will oversee the implementation of your parent's instructions. This person should have the trust of your parent and of the trust's beneficiaries, and will ideally have some skill with financial matters.

Advance Directives

In dealing specifically with issues of aging and the end of life, your loved one will need to consider such *advance directives* as *living wills* and a *durable power of attorney for health care,* also known as a *health-care proxy.* These documents specify in advance your parent's wishes regarding medical care and treatment at the end of their lives. They will communicate your parent's will in the event that, for reasons of declining health, he cannot communicate it himself.

The Living Will

The *living will* is mainly concerned with issues of the taking of heroic measures to prolong life when there is no real hope of recovery. A living will should express your loved one's thinking and decisions on the following concerns at a minimum:

- to be maintained alive by cardiopulmonary resuscitation (CPR);
- to be placed on an artificial respirator;
- to be transfused with blood and blood products;
- to undertake kidney dialysis;
- to receive food and fluids by IV or a feeding tube;
- to be withdrawn from all life-sustaining measures.

These decisions are difficult to contemplate, but they become agonizing when the moment actually comes to make them. The more you have discussed end-of-life health-care matters with your parent, the easier it will be to comply with his wishes when it is required. Talk over these issues carefully and in as much detail as possible, to ensure that your loved one's wishes will be carried out.

Power of Attorney and Health-Care Proxy

A power of attorney (POA) simply specifies a person designated by your parent as his agent, or attorney-in-fact, regarding personal and business affairs. The agent acts in your parent's stead.

For purposes of medical treatment at the end of life, your parent will need to a create a *durable* power of attorney (DPOA) for health care, also known as a *health-care proxy*, which will remain in effect until his death. This power will be invoked whenever your loved one is unable to make decisions for himself, such as for reasons of competency or anesthesia. If your parent or loved one is alive, aware, and competent, the durable power of attorney is irrelevant.

The health-care proxy names the person designated by your loved one as his attorney-in-fact — probably you, if you are the primary caregiver — as well as an alternate, in case the first choice cannot fulfill the obligation. This attorney-in-fact will have your parent's power of decision in all matters of his health care. Your parent's wishes should be openly and forthrightly discussed by her with you and your siblings, as well as the designated attorney-in-fact, to avoid any conflicts and disagreements at the eleventh hour. The terms of both the living will and the health-care proxy may be changed at any time your parent is alive and competent. State-specific advance directives may be found online at the Caring Connections website, www.caringinfo.org.

These kinds of instructions to posterity form the basic minimum set of legal documents that your parent or loved one — or for that matter, any adult, including yourself — should have had prepared and should keep readily at hand. They legally delegate responsibility for the implementation of his will regarding end-of-life decisions and the efficient disposal of his estate.

An Undesirable Alternative

Without these legal instruments, you may have to go to court to be granted the authority to implement even your loved one's most plainly stated intentions and decisions regarding her care at life's end. The process of having your parent or another loved one declared incompetent to make decisions for herself is an absolute last resort, since it may be protracted by complications such as the exact legal meaning of the concept of competency. States are reluctant to declare anyone incompetent because doing so strips the person of important legal rights — not only the right to make medical decisions, but also to vote, buy and sell property, and manage finances.

Organizing the Paperwork

You will also need to organize all of your loved one's records, documents, and paperwork. Included in this process are such things as her fundamental vital information, such as official legal name, date and place of birth (including year), bank account numbers, Social Security number and related data, passports, and driver's licenses. Additionally, you should include:

- life insurance;
- 401(k) and pension plans;
- credit cards;
- car titles and insurance policies;
- paperwork regarding her home and its maintenance;
- medical insurance;
- Medicare;
- Medicaid;
- location of safety deposits;
- titles;
- any and all relevant court documents. These items are listed on our sample Pre-Aging Agreement at the end of Chapter 3.

You will also want to note and keep handy your loved one's physicians, including all specialists and dentists, together with their addresses and contact information; the names, locations, and contact information for all pharmacies used; the name and address, with phone, of her preferred hospital; names and contact information of her neighbors and friends. Be sure to note any security codes or PINs associated with credit cards, bank accounts, insurance policies, as well as computer passwords.

Locate all legal documents relevant to your loved one(s) and make copies of each of them. You should keep one copy in a file for you and your loved one, with originals stored in a safe place.

Developing a Financial Plan

The legal matters discussed thus far all bear, one way or another, on your loved one's financial affairs. Such responsibilities should be carefully delegated to caregivers. At the outset of caregiving you will need to assess your parent or loved one's financial situation and develop a plan for her future financial security. In plain language, with your loved one's guidance and assistance, you will need to create a budget.

This process, which can become protracted depending on the extent of your parent's estate, is simple enough in its fundamentals. You and your parent begin with a frank assessment of her current assets, such as investments, real estate, savings, life insurance, and so on. Next, tally her debts, such as the mortgage on her home, outstanding loans, and any bills due. Taken altogether this data describes your parent's *net worth*, the scope within which her budget must work.

Total all sources of your parent's income (Social Security, pensions, interest on savings and investments, etc.) and then calculate all of her monthly expenses (rent and utilities, mortgages, insurance payments, and so on). Assistance with credit matters is available to you and your parent or loved one at the National Foundation for Credit Counseling at www.nfcc.org, or by calling (800) 388-2227.

Making Ends Meet

Examine her insurance policies for redundant or excessive coverage, and cancel any old policies that are no longer needed. Review her investments with her as well. Your loved one's savings may have to be used to make up any difference between her needs and her resources. Life insurance policies can be cashed in, and, if she owns a home, it may be used as collateral for a loan. Properties she owns in addition to her home may be sold. If your parent owns their home, there is even an option to apply for a reverse mortgage but only if essential funds are necessary. All potential options should be considered and explained at this point in time.

The Number 1 Priority

The critical question is how to pay for your loved one's care, which can cost from $20,000 to more than $100,000 a year in the long term. (Medicare and other such benefits will be discussed in Chapter 7 / Step 5.) This expense needs to be her and your Number 1 priority.

The two of you will need to consider other necessities as well. Does she wish to avail herself of public assistance to pay her bills, or does she intend to "go it alone"? Does she wish to set aside any sort of inheritance for her children or grandchildren? What is important *to her* in the financial realm? What are *her criteria* for financial security?

By this point, she and you should have all the information needed to create a realistic budget. Make certain that the budget is adhered to and, also, that it is reviewed periodically, or any time your loved one's material situation changes, to ensure that it is adequate to her situation.

Simplifying the Situation

Certain steps may be taken to ease and simplify your loved one's financial needs. Consolidate all of her accounts that you can, and try to locate them in a single institution if at all possible. Many sources of her income, such as Social Security and pensions, may be directly deposited into her account, eliminating some paperwork and avoiding trips to the bank. Likewise, many bills may be paid automatically by her financial institution. Finally, she may elect to sell all properties she owns other than her home.

If such an effort is beyond your loved one's management (or your own), professional money managers may be consulted and, if necessary, take over the day-to-day management of your parent's financial affairs. Costs for such services range from $25 to $75 an hour, and up. AARP also offers volunteer advice for the elderly on budgeting and money matters. These services can be accessed at AARP's financial website, www.aarpmmp.org or by calling (888) 687-2277. Help locating a professional money manager is available from the American Association of Daily Money Managers (www.aadmm.com or [301] 593-5462).

Help Is Available

The National Council on Aging also maintains a listing of programs and benefits for which your parent may be eligible at www.benefitscheckup.org. Consult as well the area agency on aging in your locality. You can find these state agencies listed in the blue pages of your phonebook.

Taxing Matters

In the realm of taxes, certain benefits accompany our aging. To begin with, some elderly citizens are not required to file federal taxes at all. Your state department of revenue may also offer certain tax benefits to the aged. People sixty-five and older receive a higher standard deduction, as well as a tax credit. Although Social Security income is taxable, your parent is exempt from most taxes on public assistance. Home improvements undertaken for medical reasons or for disabilities may be written off as medical expenses. The cost of these modifications to the home, less the property's increase in value, may be deducted from your parent's taxes. Should your loved one itemize her deductions, she may deduct all medical expenses in excess of 7.5 percent of her adjusted gross income. If her doctor orders a nursing home stay for medical reason, the entire cost may be written off.

Under certain conditions, you may be allowed to claim your parent or loved one as a dependent, though this is conditional on a yearly income of less than a few thousand dollars. Even if she does not qualify as a dependent, you may deduct any medical bills you pay if you contributed more than half of her yearly income and if those bills amounted to more than 7.5 percent of that income. If you share her expenses with siblings, you may file a *multiple support agreement* that will allow each of you to deduct the medical expenses you paid.

The Internal Revenue Service maintains a program called Tax Counseling for the Elderly that will assist your parent with his taxes at no charge. Beginning in February each year, IRS-trained volunteers, in banks, public libraries, and senior centers, assist the aged in such areas as elderly tax credits and Social Security. For more information, contact your parent's local IRS office or a center for seniors in your area. The IRS, of course, maintains a website at www.irs.gov and may be called at (800) 829-1040. AARP works in conjunction with the IRS's volunteers, counseling seniors through a program called Tax-Aide. You may call AARP at (888) 687-2277.

Confidence Men and Other Scammers

Still on the subjects of law and finances, address with your parents or loved one(s) the problem of frauds directed at the elderly. Seniors, perhaps anxious over living on a fixed income, are particularly vulnerable to any scam that promises big money fast. Loneliness and boredom also leave the aged population liable to exploitation by the unprincipled. Discuss this harsh reality with your loved one and ensure that he understands certain fundamental precautions:

- Avoid memberships and contests that promise entertainment or friendships.
- Beware of promises of easy money. If your loved one has financial difficulty, it needs to be addressed with realism, not get-rich-quick schemes.
- Never give anyone credit card or Social Security numbers unless your loved one has personally undertaken the contact.
- Donate only to respectable established charities.
- Sign up your loved one at the Do Not Call Registry at www.donotcall.gov. If telemarketers persist

in calling, complain to the Federal Trade Commission at www.ftc.gov or by calling (877) 382-4357.

- Never admit a door-to-door solicitor into the home. When responding to these visitors, keep the screen or storm door securely closed.
- Avoid contests and sweepstakes, which are almost always fraudulent.
- Pass up any "preapproved" credit card offers.
- If contacted by phone, tell the solicitor you will call his company back later — then call the business at the number listed by the phone company, not the number left over the phone.
- Refer the solicitor to your financial manager, if you employ one.
- Be prepared to cut to the chase on any sales pitches by saying, firmly and politely, "Thank you, but I am not interested."
- Apply all of the above when using the Internet or any online services. You should counsel your loved one to never give vital information (addresses, credit card or Social Security numbers) to any online site unless she personally initiated the contact. She should beware of any email from unknown sources that links her to a website which asks her to "update her account information."

Your local consumer protection agency will have even more tips for your loved ones, and you may also receive useful advice from your police department and your area agency on aging. The National Consumers League maintains a toll-free help line at (800) 876-7060. The League also hosts a website at www.fraud.org.

Also, encourage family members to make you aware of any such solicitations so you may monitor the situation.

Keeping Informed

You and your parents can keep up-to-date with the latest antics of scammers and confidence men at snopes.com, maintained by David and Barbara Michelson. Snopes contains volumes of information on frauds, hoaxes, scams, and urban legends. That email asking your father to reply with his Social Security number may already have been exposed for what it is.

If you believe that your loved one is particularly vulnerable to the lure of confidence games, you may, after discussion with her, place certain institutional barriers in place, such as a requirement for two signatures on all checks — your loved one's and yours. Your bank can also require security approval for all transactions beyond a certain amount. Maintain a small checking account for everyday expenses, and keep the bulk of your loved one's income in a separate account, to cut any losses to fraud to a minimum. Assign credit and debit cards to this minor account, so lost or stolen cards can access only a small amount of money. Of course, if competency is an issue, then your loved one's finances will have to be controlled by another person.

In the area of money and frauds, as in all relations with your parent or loved one, remain honest and open with her, encouraging her to discuss anything and everything with you at any time. Additionally, sharing this information with your siblings may be appropriate, at your mutual discretion.

CHAPTER 7 / STEP 5

Investigate benefits available

What financial assistance is available to seniors and their caregivers? How can an aging parent or loved one pay for her long-term care?

Paying for Care

The majority of people pay for their care by using a combination of private funds and benefits available under Medicare. When these alternatives are exhausted, seniors apply for help under Medicaid, the government's program for low-income citizens. Such a scenario may be avoided by a careful study of the benefits available and some advanced planning.

Private Pay and Public Assistance

Your parent or loved one bears primary responsibility for paying for her health care, to the extent that she can. This arrangement is called *private pay*. In essence, she signs a contract with her health care providers, and pays out of personal funds until money and assets are exhausted. This process may not take long, given the cost of long-term care. To protect your loved one's interests, you will need to seek the counsel of an estate planner or elder law attorney. The sooner you do this the better, since some states restrict the ways in which you can protect those interests if you have immediate need of long-term care services. An elder law attorney will be more familiar with laws relating to spending down and protecting assets.

The leading sources for the health care of the aged are the government-funded programs Medicare and Medicaid, the private insurance known as Medigap, and long-term care (LTC) insurance from private companies.

Medicare: How It Works

The U.S. Congress created Medicare in 1965 under Title XVIII of the Social Security Act, to provide publicly financed health insurance for Americans aged 65 and older. Before Medicare, only half of the U.S. elderly population had health insurance, and that half paid three times what younger citizens paid for the same insurance. The program is maintained by the Centers for Medicare and Medicaid Services (CMS), a part of the U.S. Department of Health and Human Services. Medicare is financed through a 2.9 percent payroll tax, split evenly between workers and their employers. Citizens sign up for Medicare three months before their sixty-fifth birthday.

Medicare originally consisted of two programs: one for hospital insurance, called Part A, and a second, Part B, for medical insurance. Part C, now called Medicare Advantage, was created in 1997 to allow beneficiaries to receive care from private insurers who contracted with Medicare to provide coverage. The prescription drug program, Part D, was created in 2003 and took effect on New Year's Day, 2006.

Hospital Insurance

Medicare Part A, the hospital insurance, deals with hospital stays, skilled nursing-home care, skilled health care pre-scribed by a doctor and provided in the home, hospice care, inpatient psychiatric care, and blood transfusions received as an inpatient (your parent or loved one pays for the first three pints received in a calendar year).

Hospital stays cover the first 60 days, with a copayment imposed on the next 30 days. The copay increases in the period between days 91 and 150. The basic 90-day coverage is renewed at the beginning of a new *benefit period*, which starts when the beneficiary uses neither hospital nor skilled nursing care for a period of 60 days. Barring the beginning of a new benefit period, no coverage is provided beyond 150 days. Private rooms are covered if they are deemed medically necessary, though the patient pays for any private-duty nurses.

Nursing home care is covered if the patient first spends three or more days in a hospital. Coverage pays for nurses and therapists during the first 20 days, with a copayment added for an additional 80 days. Medicine and meals are covered. Costs are not covered beyond 100 days in a given benefit period. Nor does the program pay for custodial care or private rooms.

Home health care applies to patients who are homebound. It pays for part-time or intermittent skilled care by nurses, therapists, and their aides, if prescribed by a doctor. The coverage includes both treatment and rehabilitation, and must be provided by a certified home health care company. Custodial care, such as assistance with the activities or daily living, is not covered.

Hospice care covers all medical and nursing costs, as well as medical supplies, home care, and counseling. Short-term hospitalization is covered, along with 95 percent of inpatient respite care. Drugs carry a copay of less than five dollars.

Inpatient psychiatric care is covered for 190 days in a lifetime, provided that the care is received in a free-standing psychiatric hospital.

Limiting Costs

Medicare sets limits on what it will pay for medical supplies and procedures. When a health-care supplier agrees to abide by the prices set by Medicare — an agreement known as "accepting assignment" — the patient pays the deductible as well as any coinsurance, typically 20 percent. If a doctor does not accept assignment and charges beyond the price allowed by Medicare, the patient pays the difference *as well as* the coinsurance. Do not be afraid to discuss these bills with your parent(s) doctor's billing office. Nine times out of ten they will negotiate an outstanding balance when it relates to a senior patient. Although with recent proposed changes in regards to Medicare reimbursement, sometimes the bill must be paid by the patient, who is then in turn reimbursed by Medicare.

Medicare also determines a limit on what doctors may charge in addition to the Medicare-approved amount. This limit usually allows a 15 percent increase, though there are exceptions.

Participating physicians may be found by direct inquiry with doctors' practices, with the patient's Medicare carrier, and by going to the Medicare website (www.medicare.gov) and looking in the *Participating Physician Directory*. The *Directory* may also be found at public libraries, senior centers, and Social Security offices.

Medicare Advantage

Medicare Advantage (Part C) offers additional options depending on where your parent lives. Coverage is provided by private carriers and may be broader in scope than that available under Parts A and B, though Medicare Advantage sometimes restricts the health-care providers available. Participation in Medicare Advantage has no effect on your loved one's participation in Parts A and B — she remains covered there as well. Unfortunately, because of the reduction of fees reimbursed to physicians accepting government funding, some doctors are choosing not to accept Medicare or Medicaid. Therefore, before beginning a relationship with a new physician, you may want to discuss their billing practices first and foremost.

HMOs and PPOs

Medicare Advantage offers coverage under *health maintenance organizations* (HMOs) and *preferred provider organizations* (PPOs). An HMO functions as a liaison between the insured and health care providers.

HMOs serve Medicare patients, as well as clients with other forms of health insurance. The Health Maintenance Organization Act of 1973 requires that employers with 25 or more employees who offer traditional health care benefits also offer the option of treatment in an HMO. The Medicare Modernization Act of 2003 expanded Medicare coverage to include treatment by these managed care organizations. Doctors who contract with the HMO agree to treat patients according to the HMO's guidelines and restrictions. In return, contracting physicians receive a steady stream of patients. Kaiser Medicare is a leading HMO.

Using an HMO, your loved one's care is limited to the "network" of doctors and other professional caregivers contracting with the HMO. From among these she will select a primary care physician. Should she need to see a specialist, a referral will be required from her primary care physician. She may also consult an "out-of-network" doctor, but will probably have to pay deductibles and coinsurance.

Preferred Provider Organizations, or PPOs, like Aetna and Blue Cross, offer subscription-based managed care at a discount below the regular rates of the medical professionals who participate in the PPO. In return for a constant flow of patients, the PPO receives an access fee from the participating physicians and health-care providers. The PPO negotiates the providers' fee schedules and mediates any disputes between patients and providers. PPOs target specific beneficiaries, such as nursing home patients.

PPOs operate much like HMOS, but no referral is necessary when your parent or loved one needs to see a specialist. Hospital admissions other than emergencies must satisfy a pre-certification requirement calling for prior approval by the insurer. Proposed therapies often undergo a "utilization review" to determine their appropriateness in the patient's case. Like HMOs, PPOs may charge extra for out-of-network physicians and services.

Both HMOs and PPOs agree to provide the same level of coverage as is offered by Medicare, but more offer additional options as well, including dental plans, vision plans, and audiological plans, including hearing aids.

Fee-for-Service Plans

Medicare Advantage also offers a *private fee-for-services plan* that works much like the original Medicare but has its fees, premiums, deductibles, coinsurance, and copays determined by a private carrier. Coverage extends to services provided by any Medicare-approved doctor or facility.

Medicare Advantage also offers certain "specialty" plans that provide Medicare's basic coverage with additional services covered for specific diseases and conditions, such as diabetes, congestive heart failure, and renal disease.

Medicare and Prescription Drugs

Medicare Part D, the prescription drug program, offers a number of options with varying deductibles and copays geared to what your parent can afford to pay. Basically, your parent or loved one will join a *prescription drug plan* (PDP)instead of participating in Medicare Advantage. Two-thirds of Medicare beneficiaries opt for a PDP. Not all drugs are covered at the same level, and use of lower-cost drugs is encouraged by the benefit structure. The enrollment period for Medicare Part D runs from October 15 through December 7, with a penalty for late enrollment.

As of 2012, the standard benefit offered under Part D included a $325 deductible, followed by a coinsurance payment of 25 percent up to the initial coverage limit of $2,930 for the full cost of all prescription drugs. Thereafter, the beneficiary pays the full cost of all prescriptions to a total of $4,700, at which level so-called "catastrophic coverage" begins. Under *catastrophic coverage*, beneficiaries pay either 5 percent coinsurance or $2.50 for generics and $6.30 for brand-name drugs, whichever is greater.

However, only 11 percent of patients enrolled in Part D take the standard benefit. Most plans have no deductible and use drug copays rather than coinsurance.

The Donut Hole

The gap in coverage between $2,930 and $4,700 is known as the "Donut Hole." Under the Patient Protection and Affordable Care Act of 2010, the Donut Hole gradually will be eliminated by a variety of methods, including discounts on both generic and brand-name drugs, and the gradual lowering of the $4,700 threshold for catastrophic coverage. Until then, the key is to use pharmacies that are low-cost enough to avoid ever reaching the $2,930 limit. The use of generics and volume discounts on 90-day supplies of medication from online pharmacies are two ways to stay below the Donut Hole.

In 2009, the average weighted monthly premium under Part D was $35.09. Part D does not cover drugs that are not approved by the U.S. Food and Drug Administration (FDA), nor will it provide for drugs covered under Parts A and B. The design of the program prevents the federal government from negotiating prices with pharmaceutical firms, a common practice in other federal agencies. Thus, Medicare Part D pays $785 for a year's supply of Lipitor (atorvastatin), while the U.S. Department of Veterans Affairs pays only $520 a year.

Most HMOs and PPOs also cover prescriptions, eliminating the need for Medicare Part D.

Medigap: Filling In

Medigap is a family of private supplemental policies designed to cover most or all of the deductibles and coinsurance associated with Medicare — the "gaps" in Medicare coverage. Medigap policies usually reimburse the insured for her payment of these fees. Most states limit Medigap to ten plans, labeled A through J. Medigap plans also provide coverage for copays for hospitalization, copays required under Parts A and B, the first three pints of blood transfused each year, and also covers an additional 365 days of hospitalization (lifetime) once Medicare benefits are used up.

Anticipating Needs: Medicaid

The exhaustion of Medicare benefits usually means a shift to the care of Medicaid, the government's program for people of low incomes and few assets. *You should investigate your loved one's eligibility for Medicaid well in advance of the moment of actual need.* The application process includes a review of finances in the 36 months before the patient's application for Medicaid — a specific search for any divestment of assets or money made in order to qualify for Medicaid benefits.

Medicaid, created in 1965 by the addition of Title XIX to the Social Security Act, is jointly funded by the federal government and the states. The program is managed at the state level, and you can locate your Medicaid office by contacting your local Area Agency on Aging (AAoA). These agencies operate under the Administration on Aging, which was established in 1965. Your AAoA is the local clearinghouse of information on services and programs available to seniors in your loved one's area. Housing information for seniors is also available from your local AAoA, which may be found by calling (800) 677-1116, the Eldercare Locator, or by the online search service available at www.eldercare.gov.

Medicaid Eligibility and Coverage

Who may apply for Medicaid assistance? The rules vary from state to state, but, generally speaking, Medicaid recipients are allowed to own a modest home and automobile, a prepaid funeral plan and burial plot, a small amount of savings — say, around $2,000 — and an income of only a few hundred dollars a month. This income may be derived from a job, Social Security, a pension, a retirement plan, or interest on savings. Anyone qualifying for Supplemental Security Income (SSI) automatically qualifies for Medicaid.

When investigating Medicaid, consult an attorney specializing in eldercare, who can advise you concerning the disposition of any assets that would disqualify your parent or loved one from the program. Transfer of assets to an irrevocable trust is one commonly employed answer.

Medicaid benefits are most often applied to home care. Benefits vary from state to state, but, again speaking generally, Medicaid must cover inpatient and outpatient hospital services, physician services, diagnostic tests and screenings, X-rays, lab work, services provided by rural health care clinics, medical transportation, and care provided in the home for patients who are eligible for nursing-home care.

Additionally, Medicaid may pay for prescription drugs — which coverage can help cover the costs of the Donut Hole — vision and dental, rehabilitation, prosthetics, physical therapy, and case management.

Long-Term Care Insurance

The leading alternative to the kinds of assistance discussed thus far is a rather new development in eldercare, *long-term care (LTC) insurance.* Like any insurance policy LTC insurance involves some risk that your parent will never need to access the coverage provided. On the other hand, one patient in five who uses a nursing home does so for five years or more, and, of this number, three in ten need assisted living upon leaving the nursing home. These figures translate into fairly good odds on the need for LTC coverage. The average yearly cost of nursing-home care in America is about $60,000 a year — and this figure omits therapy, rehabilitation, medications, doctor's fees, and other services as well. Yearly costs can exceed above $175,000, the average for Alaska.

Who Needs It?

The main reason to buy LTC coverage is to protect your parent's assets from exhaustion on health-care costs. Generally speaking, such policies should be purchased by:

- those with at least $100,000 in assets, exclusive of a house and all personal belongings;
- those who can pay the premiums (ranging from $300 to $600 a month or more) without exceeding 5 percent of their total yearly income.

Parents with a sizable income, or with savings in excess of $1 million, can forego LTC insurance, unless they need it for peace of mind.

Shopping Around

When looking for LTC insurance, look for providers who have been offering it for 10 years or more. Such companies have more stable rates as a result of their greater experience. The insurance offered should be flexible enough to allow for coverage of the new services stemming from advances in the field of elder medicine. Of course, your parent will want fixed premiums as well, and you should check into the company's history of rate increases. Always get everything you want in writing. A good policy also accommodates inflation, allowing for no less than 5 percent per year. You will also want a waiver of premiums when your parent is actually receiving long-term care. Check this clause in your policy carefully for any limitations on the length or type of long-term care provided with a waiver of premiums. Also, assure that the policy covers dementia, Alzheimer's, and any other forms of "organic brain disease." The policy should be guaranteed renewable and protected against cancellation (LTC policies should be cancelled only for non-payment of premiums or falsification of application). You will also want an initial period of 30 days during which the policy may be cancelled by your parent or loved one with a full refund.

Benefits Available to Veterans

Veterans of the armed forces have a wide range of health-care benefits available to them from the U.S. Department of Veterans Affairs (VA).

Under the VA Aid and Attendance program, for instance, married veterans who served during wartime are eligible to receive up to $22,104 of tax-free income yearly to pay one person to assist them with an activity of daily living. The veteran need only to have served during wartime; actual participation in combat is not the requirement. Single veterans can receive $18,648 yearly. The assistance may be provided by friends, family, neighbors, or professionals, and veterans residing in assisted living facilities are automatically eligible.

VA pensions range from $985 to $1949 a month for those qualified. Retired career military personnel are eligible for expanded medical coverage known as TRICARE. You may learn more about TRICARE by calling (888) 363-2273 or by visiting the website at www.tricareonline.com.

Most veterans not receiving VA disability compensation or pension payments must provide information on their gross annual household income and net worth to determine whether they are below annually adjusted financial thresholds. This financial assessment includes all household income and net worth, including Social Security, retirement pay, unemployment insurance, interest and dividends, workers' compensation, black lung benefits and any other income. Also considered are assets such as the market value of property other than the veteran's home, stocks, bonds, notes, individual retirement accounts, bank deposits, savings accounts and cash. The VA income thresholds are located at www4.va.gov.healtheligibility/Library/AnnualThresholds.asp .

Other benefits include burial in national cemeteries, inscribed headstones, and funeral services with full military honors. You may investigate what is available to your parent or loved one by calling the VA at (800) 827-1000 or by accessing the agency's website at www.va.gov. A 135-page guide, *Federal Benefits for Veterans, Dependents and Survivors* is available from the VA as a free download at www.va.gov/opa/publications/benefits_book/federal_benefits.pdf

Privacy Issues and HIPAA

Privacy will be an issue in your loved one's medical care. You will want to maintain a complete copy of all her medical records, and you will need legal permission to do this. In 1996 the U.S. Congress passed *the Health Insurance Portability and Accountability Act (HIPAA)*. This law, meant primarily to prevent employers and insurance providers from imposing pre-existing conditions clauses, also addresses ensures of patient privacy. The HIPAA privacy standards underlie the lines that are set at some distance from the counters of pharmacies, which distancing assures you of private counsel with your pharmacist. But the law also imposes conditions on the privacy of personal medical information. HIPAA rules do not require a written statement of permission to enable you to view your loved one's medical records, but your health-care provider may want the legal security of such a document on file in his office.

An understanding of HIPAA regulations can prevent difficulties accessing medical information on your parent at a later date. Frequently Asked Questions concerning the ins and outs of HIPAA may be accessed by category or keyword search at http://www.hhs.gov/ocr/privacy/hipaa/faq/index.html.

One Thing at a Time

The amount of paperwork associated with caregiving for an aging parent or loved one is truly staggering. You will find it best to take this task on in a methodical, step-by-step way. Work on one thing at a time, and feel free to spread out the work on the dining room table or the living room floor. Make a file for everything, so when mail and paperwork arrive, you immediately file it in the proper folder. Trust me – when you begin receiving mounds upon mounds of paperwork, this system truly will preserve your sanity. If you begin to feel overwhelmed, take a break, go for a walk, call a friend, or do something good for yourself. Recall the answer to the riddle, "How do you eat an elephant?" One bite at a time.

Everything Is Negotiable

Finally, understand that everything concerning your loved one's health care is negotiable. Resourcefulness and diligence should be your watchwords in navigating the sea of benefits available for the care of your parent or loved one. Alternatives exist to any *no* you may encounter.

CHAPTER 8 / STEP 6

Review medical care and medications

What issues do you as a caregiver need to address concerning medical care and medications?

Gathering More Information

The answer concerning medication begins with an upfront discussion between you and your parent or loved one concerning her doctors — she will probably use more than one — and each physician prescribing a different medication.

Selecting a Physician

Identify all the physicians who contribute to her care. Get names and numbers, and any other relevant contact information she can give you, and write all this all down. In reviewing her medications, note which doctor prescribed what drugs, and note his prescriptions beside his name. List the medicines by brand name and drug name, when possible, along with the dosage instructions and the quantities and dosages in which the medicines are prescribed.

Your loved one may have a family doctor with whom she feels comfortable. If such is not the case, and often it is not, you and she will have to undertake together a search for an acceptable physician to function as her primary care provider (PCP).

This job is an important one. All of your loved one's medical care, including prescription information, will be communicated to and overseen by her PCP. This doctor may be a general practitioner or a specialist in geriatric medicine. The important thing is that the physician has your loved one's respect, trust, and confidence, that he (or she) be someone with whom your loved one feels free to discuss any aspect of her healthcare. This physician is the one who is in charge of your loved one's care, the final arbiter of all decisions made concerning her health and well being.

Diversity and Other Issues

Finding a physician so qualified may be a challenge. His (or her) personality and rapport with your parent or loved one may be the deciding factors, rather than a diploma from a prestigious medical school. Is your loved one more comfortable with a physician of her own gender? Are race or ethnicity issues for her? Medicine is international today — how would she feel about using a foreign doctor? How does she feel about a young doctor, as opposed to someone with decades of experience? Which is more important to her, technical expertise or personal warmth?

You might ask your own personal physician for some recommendations. Ask your friends, siblings, and neighbors as well. Such word of mouth is often the best of all recommendations. You may also inquire at the referral departments of local hospitals, as well as among the staff of any local senior centers.

Your choice may be limited by Medicare or other insurance requirements to employ in-network practitioners. Not all doctors accept Medicare or Medicaid, and some will only be accessible through an HMO.

In lieu of personal recommendations, you may investigate the licensure and malpractice and other issues concerning candidate doctors on your state government's website. This site is typically the state's two-letter postal abbreviation, followed by the domain ".gov." The New York state government site, for example, is www.ny.gov.

A Brief Guide to Consultations

You will want to settle on a primary care provider as early as possible in the caregiving process. It will almost certainly take a while to find a good fit, and you do not need to be pressed by the demands of a medical crisis on your loved one's part while searching for this doctor. It may also take weeks for a new patient to get an appointment, and both you and she will need some time to get to know the new physician, and to have all relevant medical records forwarded to his practice.

You will want to accompany your loved one to her first visit with her PCP, and you need to know whether he is comfortable with your presence in the examination room. If your loved one has difficulty hearing or is frequently confused by medical technicalities, it may be advisable for you to accompany her into the exam for the sake of clear understanding. Most physicians will field such requests on a case-by-case basis.

Whatever the doctor's decision regarding your presence during consultations, you should develop your own relationship with your loved one's PCP. Cultivate an open and honest understanding of each other and of your role in your loved one's medical care. You do not need a physician who cannot be forthcoming with you on such matters. Be equally direct with him: do not let yourself be intimidated by the doctor's profession. Do not hesitate to ask for explanations of diagnoses and treatments, and speak up if you feel the physician is slighting your loved one's care in any way. Remain free to switch to another PCP if you believe a switch to be desirable and necessary; do not worry about the doctor's feelings. You are not there to take care of him. It is also important for you to understand the availability of the doctor. Will your family member be "his" patient alone or be seen by another physician in his group? This may cause confusion at a later date.

These days, practices are being consolidated, sometimes with up to 70 doctors practicing together. Make sure you as the caregiver understand how each practice is set up before committing your loved one(s) to their care.

Given the state of American health care today, your loved one may not often see her PCP, but will have her needs attended to instead by a Nurse Practitioner (NP) or a Physician's Assistant (PA). If so, these staff need to satisfy the criteria above if they are to serve effectively and well in the place of your PCP.

Remember that some issues of patient privacy lie beyond the reach of the HIPAA rules discussed earlier. Your loved one has a right to discuss her health care privately with her doctor, and, if she elects, to keep the information from you and the rest of the family, although you do not wish to encourage this confidentiality, primarily due to the fact that you are acting as their caregiver and need to understand all aspects of your loved one(s) medical situation to offer the best medical care possible.

When you do get to see the doctor, remember to schedule appointments at times convenient for your loved one, not yourself. Accompany her to the practice, and be prepared for a long wait. You may be called early, but you should not count on it. Bring books to read or something else that will help each of you pass the time. Patience is not the long suit of small children and teenagers, so do not include them in your trips to the doctor.

The First Visit

On the first visit, you and your loved one will need to inform her PCP of certain items:

- history of illnesses, test, and hospitalizations;
- any surgeries;
- any current symptoms;
- medications currently prescribed, by whom and for what;
- vitamins and other over-the-counter remedies in use;
- allergies, to nature and to medicines;
- daily habits (eating, sleeping, etc.);
- any problems with any activity of daily living;
- any family history of illness, physical or mental/emotional;
- any substance use or abuse (tobacco, alcohol, etc.);
- names and contact information of previously consulted physicians;
- all medical records.

Attending your loved one's visits to her physician will familiarize you in some depth with her health care issues. Of course, you may be asked to leave the office, and if so, you will step outside, but usually you will attend the visit with your loved one and physician, and so become increasingly informed about her medical situation. My own father always wanted me present at all appointments. Going to see the doctor together gave us an opportunity to review, after we left the appointment, what the physician had said to us. We were both completely informed as to his medical situation, and therefore we could each accurately convey concerns and issues to other family members or friends. We were all "on the same page," unlike with my mother, who attended all doctor visits on her own, which somewhat kept our family in the dark about pressing conditions. Also, since she was seeing a variety of physicians, each prescribing different medications, and not communicating with each other, there were times when drugs were not interacting properly together, causing great concern.

When you do see the physician, or the PA or NP, be succinct and to-the-point with him, and encourage your loved one to do likewise. Begin the encounter with a simple statement of the primary reason for the visit. Bring with you a list of symptoms and anything else relevant to the case. Absent any outward, obvious symptoms on your loved one's part, such communication is the only way the doctor will know what he needs to address.

Cultivate good listening skills and take detailed notes. *Ask questions.* Be sure you understand the doctor's answers, and if in doubt about anything, *ask more questions.*

Understanding Prescriptions

Be sure as well that you and your loved one understand the treatments and medicines your doctor prescribes. Again, always ask questions. In the case of prescription drugs, some questions will always apply:

- What is this medicine for, and why is he taking it?
- How long does my parent need to take this medication?

- How many times a day should he take this medicine, and how should he take it (with or without food, etc.)?
- Does the medicine have any side effects for which we should watch? If so, what are they and how should we respond to them?
- Does the medicine treat his problem symptomatically, or does it address the cause directly?
- Will the drug act immediately or will it take some time?
- Could this drug interact poorly with any other medications he is taking?
- What should he do if he misses a dose?
- How soon will he respond to this therapy?
- Should he continue taking the medicine once the condition is resolved?
- How much does this medicine cost?
- Is the medicine available in generic form?

As you can see from the nature of these questions, you will need to know everything possible about your loved one's current state of health and medications in use. Your knowledge of his medical history can be critical in the event of an emergency — existing conditions, surgeries, drug and other allergies, and medications taken and prescribed. You are wise to have such information up-to-date and in summary written form, along with a list of all his health-care providers, together with their contact information and the nature of the specific health issues they address. All of this critical data can be managed in your medical folder.

Maintaining a Comprehensive Medical Record

All communication from medical professionals attending your loved one should be forwarded to the primary caregiver, assumed here to be you. This information, along with copies of all records of care, should also be forwarded to your loved one's PCP, who will maintain a unified and comprehensive record of his medical care. Of course, keep all family members informed of your loved one's medical situation. This information may be distributed by email to a list, on a family blog, or on an individual, one-to-one basis. The point is that no one will be left in the cold, and all concerned will be on the same page.

Your loved one's PCP also will have final authority on what therapies may be undertaken by your parent, and which medicines may be prescribed for him. Any specialists your loved one may consult will assume that someone — likely, you — has her thoughts on the big picture and is keeping all other practitioners informed.

Effects of Diet on Medication

Review your loved one's diet with her PCP, with an eye to any foods that may interact badly with the medicines she is taking. Do the same for any vitamins and alternative remedies she uses. Double check her prescription medications for any that impede the absorption of vitamins and minerals. When in any doubt, ask her PCP. My dad, for instance, couldn't eat grapefruit because of a drug interaction.

At Your Pharmacy

Here are some questions to be asked of your loved one's pharmacist as well:

- Is there a less expensive generic equivalent of this medicine that works just as well?
- Is there a comparable medicine that works as well as the one prescribed, but available at a savings?
- Does the medicine have special storage requirements (refrigeration, stored in darkness, etc.)?
- How can the medicine be taken? Must it be swallowed whole, or can it be broken up, or powdered and mixed with food and water? If in capsule form, can the capsule be emptied into a glass of milk? Is the medicine available in liquid form?
- Can the pharmacist review the dosage instructions with you?

Try to conduct all your pharmaceutical business with a single pharmacy if at all possible. If you can, then you will have access to a pharmacist with full, computerized knowledge of what drugs and treatments are currently prescribed for your parent. Such a pharmacist can sometimes alert you and your loved one to the prescription by one specialist of medicine that is contraindicated by the treatment from a second doctor.

Saving Money

When a new medicine is prescribed, have the pharmacist dispense a limited number as a sample. Once you are sure your loved one tolerates and responds to the medicine, then buy the number prescribed. Ask the pharmacist whether the drug is available at lower prices in bulk quantities. Compare prices with mail-order online pharmacies. If the savings is substantial, a distant supplier may be the one to use. Many states and localities offer special prescription drug discount programs to seniors. Some commercial outlets also employ such discounts to build their customer base. If your loved one is a veteran of the armed forces, the medication may be available at a considerable savings through the VA drug plan.

Information on Prescription Drugs

Medicare maintains an online data base of prescription drug assistance programs at www.medicare.gov, also accessible by calling 800-MEDICARE. Additional information on such discounts may be found at the following websites:

- National Council on Aging,
  www.benefitscheckuprx.com
- Partnership for Prescription Assistance,
  www.pparx.org
- Volunteers in Health Care RxAssist,
  www.rxassist.org

A Pill Box and Other Aids

Once prescriptions are settled, impress your loved one with the importance of following dosage instructions, and buy her a pill box designed to reinforce her schedule. These may be as simple as a seven-compartment box for medicines taken once a day, or a larger one that breaks out the days of the week into time periods such as Morning, Noon, and Evening. Whatever you decide upon, ensure that the box is filled on a regular basis and that your loved one adheres to the schedule. These are available at most drug stores.

If necessary, you may wish to create a chart for your loved one's daily schedule of medicines. Such a chart would be broken out across the waking hours of the day. Each medicine would be listed, along with its dosage instructions and any additional directions for its use. Your loved one then checks off each dose at its appropriate time. The schedule would have to be replaced with a fresh chart on a regular basis, perhaps daily. Include any vitamin supplements and naturopathic therapies in the schedule as well. Try to make the schedule easy to read and to work with, and avoid any overly complicated designs.

Monitor your loved one's supplies of medicines and expiration dates, vitamins, and alternative therapies to ensure that she does not run out of anything. Some pharmacies have programs that allow for prescriptions to be refilled automatically, with a call made to the patient to remind her. Ask your pharmacist whether he offers any such service. Most importantly, as we age we sometimes wind up taking a wide variety of medications, vitamins, and supplements. Do not add anything new to the mix without clearance from your parent's attending physician. One small addition may result in unplanned serious consequences. Also, when prescribed any new medication, monitor all positive and negative reactions, and report back to your parent's doctor for further examination and discussion.

Finally, you will also want to keep a close eye on any medical equipment on which your loved one relies, such as walkers, canes, wheelchairs, beds, and any devices you have installed in the home to assist her in her daily activities, such as grab bars, raised toilet seats and commodes, night lights, as well as oxygen equipment. A dysfunctional piece of equipment can result in a devastating injury.

CHAPTER 9 / STEP 7

Establish a maintenance plan

What can you routinely expect as the primary caregiver for an aging parent? What sort of things ordinarily will confront you?

Activities of Daily Living

Your parent's *activities of daily living* (ADLs) include a range of ordinary tasks such as bathing and grooming, dressing, cooking and eating, getting around (mobility), and sleeping. Your parent's ability or inability to perform these seemingly simple acts provides you with a measure of the extent, and limitations, of his abilities.

The more structured his day is, the better. For example, knowing each day that breakfast is from 7:00 to 9:00 a.m., lunch from 12:00 to 2:00 p.m., and dinner from 5:00 to 7:00 p.m. is very helpful. Bath days are Tuesday, Thursday, and Saturday at 8:00 a.m. Therapy is Monday, Wednesday, Friday at 10:00 a.m. Such a weekly schedule, posted in a handy place, keeps the senior focused on each day at hand. You can assist him in "filling in the blanks" with other visits and activities. It is a simple, easy system that works.

Bathing and Grooming

Good hygiene is essential to feeling good, and *bathing and grooming* — caring for yourself and your appearance — are fundamental to self-esteem. Such activities, however, can be difficult for an aging parent. Your job as a caregiver is to ensure that your parent cares for himself as much and as well as he can, and to assist him in any areas where his abilities are limited.

Bathing — getting in and out of the shower or tub — can be tricky for older people. Chapter 5 / Step 3 discussed some of the physical modifications to the bathroom that can ease such difficulties for your parent. Grab bars, nonskid mats, and tub chairs are among the devices that you will probably need to install.

Skin Care

In the bath or shower itself, we care for our body's largest organ, *skin*. Water constitutes 55 percent of the human body, and our skin maintains these fluids, all essential to the function of the human organism. Care of the skin is critical among the elderly, because skin loses elasticity with age and grows dryer and thinner. Old skin needs careful applications of moisturizers.

Aged skin, thin and weak, leaves your parent, when confined to a bed or a wheelchair spending a lot of time in one position, especially susceptible to bedsores. Continuous pressure on a given area of skin inhibits blood flow, and skin starved of this most essential bodily fluid becomes scarred and red, displaying blisters and open sores. Certain simple steps may be taken to address this risk to bedridden parents.

- Reposition your parent every hour or so, and, if he can, have him slightly shift his position in his bed or wheelchair even more often.
- Movement stimulates the flow of blood, so have him stand up or spend some time sitting in a chair if he can. If he cannot leave the bed have him engage in whatever movement he can manage — wiggling his toes, bending his legs, waving his arms.
- Change bedsheets and clothing regularly to help keep skin clean and dry.
- Top off his mattress with an egg-crate foam mattress, which forms a cushion for him and relieves some of the pressure of his weight.
- Gently massage him to stimulate his circulation, as well as to improve his mood.
- Be alert to signs of redness, which can signal pending troubles.
- Always consult a physician if the situation worsens.

Common Complaints

Other common skin complaints among the elderly include itching and fungal infections. Consider the following general steps to maintain the health of your parent's skin:

- Have him take only two or three baths a week, and make them short and warm rather than long and hot. Heat and water dry out human skin.
- Use glycerin soap with cleansing cream, and apply moisturizer while drying off, when the skin is still somewhat damp. On particularly dry spots, use petroleum jelly.

- Do not scrub the skin harshly.
- Cotton is easier on skin than wool or synthetic fabrics. Have your parent wear loose-fitting clothing that breathes, allowing air to circulate through it.
- Have him drink plenty of fluids — but avoid alcohol and caffeine, along with tobacco and spicy foods.
- Try calamine lotion on particularly troublesome itching, and contact a doctor or dermatologist at the first sign of any bleeding.
- Over-the-counter antifungals are fine for everyday use.
- Consult a physician at any sign of *stasis dermatitis*, when the skin becomes dry, cracked, and discolored with red-brown patches of itching purple spots.

Foot Rest — and Care

Pay attention to the condition of your parent's *feet*, and take proper steps to treat calluses, corns, bunions, general infections, and any sores that inhibit his movement. Wash his feet daily, and apply lanolin or other moisturizers to dry areas on the feet. Trim his nails often and treat him to a pedicure. Be sure his shoes fit. Foot massages improve the flow of blood, as do walking and general exercise. Check his feet regularly and closely for cuts, abrasions, and minor injuries in general. If he has diabetes, take particular care with his feet, because this disease can seriously affect blood flow and put his extremities at special risk.

Dental Care and a Healthy Mouth

Dental hygiene should be high on your list of priorities. People sixty-five and older suffer from more tooth decay than any other age group, so your elderly parent needs special attention to the care of his teeth and gums. He should see his dentist at least once a year, and brush and floss his teeth at least twice a day. Bad teeth can interfere with eating and adversely affect his nutrition. Inform his dentist of any health problems he has, as well as any medications or treatments that other physicians prescribe for him.

If he wears *dentures*, have them checked regularly and refitted as necessary. His gums, tongue, and the inside of his mouth need regular brushing to freshen his breath.

Dry mouth is not simply a by-product of aging. If your parent complains of dryness, bring it to the attention of his dentist and his doctor. Temporary relief may be found with cough drops and chewing gum, preferably free of sugar.

Other tips for a healthy mouth include:

- Use a toothpaste with fluoride to fight decay.
- Employ flossing tools that make the floss easier for your parent to handle and manipulate.
- If you brush his teeth for him, have his dental hygienist demonstrate the proper techniques.
- If he has difficulty swallowing, don't use toothpaste or he may choke on the foam. A wet brush or a damp cloth will do the job adequately.

Sight and Sore Eyes

Care must be taken with aging *eyes* as well. *Presbyopia*, a common problem beginning in the forties and progressing from there, makes it difficult for us to see small print or objects that are close. The usual remedy is a pair of reading glasses.

We also begin to see less well in dim light as we age. We are more susceptible to glare and cannot refocus, from light to darkness or from far to near, as quickly as we could when young. Illuminate the house well and thoroughly and cut down on bright spots by covering or removing reflective surfaces. A pair of sunglasses with protection from ultraviolet radiation will also reduce the effect of glare. If night vision is a problem for him, position night-lights in his bedroom, the bath, and hallways.

A range of *vision aids* can help your parent to see, including magnifying glasses, large-print books, and large-print devices such as calculators and phones. Some telephone companies offer dialing help and operator assistance for the visually impaired. You can shop online for vision aids at the National Foundation of the Blind (www.nfb.org) and the National Association for the Visually Handicapped (www.navh.org). Your public library will have copies of large-print editions of popular books, as well as abridged and unabridged audio books.

Common Eye Problems

Most common eye diseases that can afflict your parent include:

- *Cataracts,* which cloud the transparent lens of the eye, often form so gradually that your parent may not notice that anything is going wrong. Surgery may become necessary, and relieves the condition in 90 percent of all cases.
- *Glaucoma* can lead to blindness, partial and total, as the optic nerve is damaged by a build-up of fluid inside the eye. Medications can slow or stop the

damage, and a successful laser surgery technique has been developed. More traditional surgery may also be employed.

- *Age-related macular degeneration* breaks down the part of the retina that clarifies fine details at the center of the field of vision, leading to a blind spot there. The condition can deteriorate to the point that your parent cannot see the words in the middle of his visual field, and the time may come when all central vision is lost. There is no cure, but therapies exist which slow the progress of the condition.

- *Diabetic retinopathy*, the leaking of blood vessels in the eye, can cause blindness if not treated, and the chances of developing the problem increase the longer an aging parent suffers from diabetes. The most effective therapy is proper treatment for the diabetes.

Losing your eyesight is very frightening, especially to an elderly adult, therefore make sure your parent has regular eye exams.

Hearing and Hearing Aids

Hearing loss can mark the coming of age as well. *Presbycusis* is a common problem, also known as *sensorineural hearing loss*, or hearing impairment due to nerve damage. In this condition the *volume* of sound is detected correctly but *clarity* is lost — your parent can hear others, but does not understand what they are saying. Presbycusis is thought to be a normal part of aging.

Another source of hearing trouble is *tinnitus*, a high-pitched ringing or buzzing in the ears that can also manifest as clicking or hissing sounds. Tinnitus may or may not have a treatable cause. If your parent's case does not, an audiologist can often find way to relieve the condition.

Various systems may be employed to amplify sound, and silent alarms can provide visual signals of ringing doorbells and telephones, chiming clocks, and smoke detectors. Tactile signals such as vibration may also be employed.

Changes in hearing should be addressed by an otologist or an otolaryngolist, doctors who specialize in hearing disorders. An audiologist may be consulted if there is nothing physically wrong with your parent's ear, and this specialist can assess the degree of hearing loss, fit your parent with a hearing aid, and show him how best to use it.

Your parent will need help in adjusting to life with a hearing aid. Many older people actively resist such therapy. Explain to your parent that advances in technology have improved hearing aids dramatically. Today's models are almost unnoticeable.

After a check-up to make certain that your parent's hearing loss is not an infection, blockage, or other physically treatable problem, have him consult an audiologist. Find one who can devote a lot of time to your parent's case, for even with improved technology, the fit of a hearing aid can vary widely from one person to another.

A Selection of Hearing Aids

The least expensive hearing aids simply amplify all sound equally. Selectivity is not possible. These models do not emulate the human ear: they will not tune out background noise and focus on the conversation in the foreground.

Next are models that allow for such selectivity, with settings adjustable according to the environment — a dinner table in the evening or a baseball stadium on a Sunday afternoon. Digital versions of such hearing aids can analyze the audal environment and adjust themselves, but you will pay a pretty penny for such devices. Implantable hearing aids, costing several thousand dollars, can often improve hearing loss due to nerve damage, such as presbycusis. Most expensive — more than $50,000 — are cochlear implants for elderly people who are profoundly deaf.

A period of adjustment will be necessary for your parent no matter how fine an instrument he selects. See if you can get him to commit to a three-month trial, one day at a time, and encourage him to revisit his hearing specialist with any and all difficulties he encounters.

Meals, Dining, and Nutrition

Meals can pose problems for the elderly, who must learn to cook for one or two after a lifetime spent raising an entire family. Your parent may easily come to rely on processed and frozen foods in lieu of really nutritious meals. In prepared foods, look for the low-sodium and low-fat varieties, and encourage the use of herbs and spices to add flavor to an otherwise rather bland meal. If you are preparing the food for your loved one, give some thought to preparing small servings and then freezing them for later warm-up and consumption. We discuss other options in Chapter 5 / Step 3.

Proper *nutrition*, of course, is essential to well-being at any age. Public health experts recommend a diet rich in whole-grain foods like brown rice and wheat bread. Serve fruit several times each day, and supply protein with several daily servings of fish, poultry, or eggs. Other elements of a healthy diet include nuts and legumes up to three times a day, and a dairy product, preferably low in fat, or calcium supplement several times a day. Red meat, butter, white rice and pasta, soft drinks, and sweets should be consumed only sparingly. Taking a multivitamin daily is also a good idea, if approved by your family physician. Also, it is important to watch for any reactions when eating certain foods.

Kitchen Safety

Safety in the kitchen is an issue as well. Many seniors forget to turn off the stove or oven, so post reminders in the kitchen to discourage forgetfulness. A smoke alarm is an essential in the home of any aged parent. Position it just outside the kitchen to avoid false alarms. A number of counter-top appliances can replace the use of the large oven and stove-top, and encourage the preparation of small servings of food.

A little reorganization can also help make the kitchen a safer place. Place frequently used items in easy-to-reach locations, to spare your parent from climbing stepladders and standing on chairs, as well as avoiding deep-knee bends and, I know this sounds silly, but familiarity is very important as we age. My own father knew exactly what was on each shelf of the refrigerator. Heaven forbid I should move the milk to the second shelf when it clearly belongs on the first! We may make light of this, but it is important to keep things in their place and clean out our parent's refrigerator weekly. If not, you may find unwanted mold growing on the lettuce and find out-dated cream or other several-week-old leftovers, all causing a potential source of illness.

Getting Around

Most elderly people experience some difficulty with *personal mobility.* We reach an age when we just do not get around like we used to. This situation can result from pain related to movement, a deteriorating sense of balance, and simple fear of falling.

If pain is inhibiting movement, consult your parent's PCP regarding pain management. Balance may be an inner ear problem, either a build-up of wax or an infection. Just be patient and take things slowly, one step at a time. Rushing can only cause stress and accidents.

Elder Exercise

Exercise can limber up your parent a bit, and this will improve his sense of balance and boost his confidence and self-esteem. A simple set of range-of-motion exercises can involve most of his muscles, and can be performed even while lying in bed. These involve things like rotating your head in a circle; shrugging your shoulders and raising them singly, one at a time; lifting one arm, and then the other, over your head; making small circles with your wrists as you sit with your arms at your sides; touching the base of your little finger several times with the tip of your thumb; raising your feet off the floor and then "going on point" like a ballerina; and drawing clockwise circles in the air with your big toe, then redrawing them counter-clockwise.

Of course, more strenuous exercises will yield bigger benefits, such as increased mobility and improved levels of energy and stamina. Just walking every day gets your loved one out of the house and into the sunshine, and is a real stimulant against depression. Feeling better generally will lead to reduced anxiety and less worry about health. Exercise also improves balance, a big plus among the elderly, where slips and falls can spell disaster. Existing physical conditions, such as heart disease and diabetes respond positively to increases in exercise.

Have your loved one discuss an exercise plan with her PCP, who can develop a regimen appropriate to her case. If possible, encourage her to join a gym or the Y, and check out nearby community-based programs. Not only will the exercise be a positive influence on their health, it will also serve as extended socialization and "a time and a place to go," bringing some refreshing order to their lives.

Once my dad enrolled in a community gym, he went every day at 3:00 p.m. The activity gave him a new purpose and social experience, not to mention something to talk about with his family and friends. He even brought his neighbor as his guest, every Sunday. He became more mobile, slept better at night, and, additionally, his vital signs improved. It was a total positive experience for him.

Aerobic exercises such as walking, riding a bicycle, swimming, and other aquatic exercise works out the heart and lungs and can lead to improved endurance. Strength exercises, designed to build muscle, will lead to improved general strength and metabolism, and lessen the risk of osteoporosis. Range of motion exercise, such as bending and stretching, increase your loved one's flexibility while relieving tension and easing the pains of arthritis. Such activities will get your loved one out of the house, and will lead to improved sleep and better rest.

Sleep, Deep and Otherwise

Your parent may or may not *sleep* less as he grows older, but he will definitely sleep lighter, and may consequently feel less rested. All the factors that disrupt healthy sleep — depression and stress, inactivity and lack of exercise, pain, diet, and so on — can intensify with age. Your parent should avoid alcohol, tobacco, and caffeine. Coffee, if consumed at all, should be a morning drink, not an after-dinner one. A glass of wine or a jigger of whiskey will likely cause your father to wake up in the middle of the night as the alcohol wears off; but a warm glass of milk is a natural tranquilizer. Certain medications can interfere with sleep — diuretics, decongestants, steroids, antihypertensives, and drugs used to treat Parkinson's. Some antidepressants also may have a stimulating effect. Review all of your parent's medications with his PCP and eliminate those that may be disrupting his rest. Good rest is essential to feeling good about each new day.

The Secret to a Good Night's Rest

The secret key to a good night's sleep, though, is a busy day — as busy as your parent can comfortably handle. Sitting bored in an easy chair drifting off while "watching" television all day is not going to lead to solid, restful sleep at night. And, as we age our sleep patterns change. We may stay up later and rise later in the morning, or vice versa. Whatever pattern works well for your parent is acceptable, as long as they are getting the rest they need.

Help your parent find things to do during the day. Ask for his help with chores like sorting laundry or gardening, matching clean socks or clipping coupons. A hobby may absorb his interest and pass the time with a feeling of accomplishment. If he can, he should take regular walks. Sometimes, if the weather is threatening, a walk through the local indoor shopping mall would work just fine. I remember my grandmother would walk three times a week at the mall near her home in Florida, first thing in the morning before all the shops would open. When I came with her one morning, I had no idea she had company . . . there were at least 100 other "senior walkers!"

He should limit his nap time to no more than thirty minutes in the middle of the afternoon. Using the bathroom just before retiring will aid sound sleep, and he should avoid drinking fluids late in the day. The antihistamine diphenhydramine, often marketed as allergy medicine, can aid him in falling to sleep, as can the various over-the-counter "PM" pain medicines. Above all, if he does not get to sleep after twenty minutes or so, he needs to get up and do something — read a book, watch a video, or even write a letter — because literally anything is better than lying awake in bed worrying about his lack of sleep.

Addressing Incontinence

Thirty percent of the elderly experience *incontinence,* either partial or complete, and this figure rises to 50 percent among the hospitalized population of aged people. The sphincter muscle loses strength in old age, and this can lead to awkward and embarrassing situations. Acknowledging the problem in the first place may be the most significant barrier to addressing it, but if you approach the subject gently and with tact, steps can be taken to resolve the difficulty.

Consult your parent's PCP or other doctor, and if you find no help — research shows that 50 percent of doctors fail to respond to requests for help with incontinence — consult a urologist, gastroenterologist, or geriatrician.

Exercises and Training

Urinary incontinence may be addressed with exercises and bladder training, which almost always relieve the problem. The training involves visiting the bathroom every hour or so and making a conscious effort to urinate. Kegel exercises, which strengthen the ring of muscle around the bladder's exit tube, can also help. The exercise involves squeezing the muscles of the vagina and anus. These are the muscles employed to stop the flow of urine, and they may be squeezed discreetly, without attracting any attention; Kegel exercises will need to be done several hundred times a day for at least a month before your parent experiences their effect. Like all exercise, Kegels call for discipline.

Bed pans and mobile commodes are options for the physically-impaired parent who has difficulty reaching the bathroom in time. These may be placed beside his bed or chair. If at all possible, his bedroom should give easy access to the bathroom.

Your parent may find bowel training, the parallel to the treatment for urinary incontinence, a harder discipline to follow, but usually we have established some sort of regular pattern of elimination in our lives, and the exercises can draw on this experience to respond to bowel incontinence.

Diapers and incontinence pads catch accidents and protect clothes and furniture from soiling. A possible drawback to this response is that your parent may stop all efforts at exercise and self-control, lapsing into dependence on the diapers and pads. But he is just as likely to use them to train himself, and employed in this way, they can be a great aid.

Diapers can also chafe, promoting rashes and skin infections. No one should remain in a soiled diaper any longer than is necessary. At changing time, clean the soiled area with mild soap and water, dried off with a cotton towel. Apply moisturizer to help prevent irritation. Most diapers can be purchased at any drug store, or in larger quantities at Target or Wal-mart. They may also be delivered in bulk to your parent's door by checking out binsons.com on the Web. They offer many discounts and free shipping. Just remember this is a somewhat embarrassing and delicate issue, so choose your words carefully.

Catheters

The very last resort, the Foley *catheter*, has the drawback of promoting urinary infections, which means that the device must be frequently changed. A catheter is simply a tube inserted into your parent's bladder that carries urine to a waste receptacle suspended under his bed or hidden under his clothing. They are commonly used with patients confined to a bed or wheelchair.

Diet and Incontinence

Bowel incontinence may also be addressed by switching your parent to a diet high in fiber. The exercises applied to the problem of urinary incontinence all apply here as well. It may be helpful to have your parent sit on the toilet for a while each morning after a breakfast that stimulates the bowels. To empty the bowels on a regular schedule, use enemas and suppositories. These are most useful when nerve damage results in incontinence by preventing the occurrence of the sensations that normally alert a person to the onset of a bowel movement. Certain drugs may also be employed, such as stool-bulking agents which counteract loose stool.

The Importance of a Social Life

Socialization is a meaningful necessity of human life at any age. Simply talking with other members of the household, whether it be the caregiver's home or a skilled nursing facility, satisfies a real human need. If your parent is competent with a computer, e-mail and family-centered blogs can expand his social circle.

A senior center is a good place to start looking for activities that will draw your loved one out of the house and into the world. Most offer group programs that encourage the elderly to share common interests.

Aging also offers an improved opportunity to volunteer in the community. Suggest that your loved one investigate possibilities at the local library, a nearby hospital or nursing home, school, or church. At 80, my in-laws volunteered at a local nursing home – go figure!

A part-time job may also be a possibility for some seniors, and adult education is an avenue also worth pursuing - many community arts centers offer courses in pottery, drawing, painting, stained glass, photography, feng shui, and more.

Socialization with other age groups is always an insightful experience. Having your parents at a pre-school or middle school function, or at a teenager's birthday party, can be a welcome change from the constant company of other elderly friends. It opens up their world into a wider spectrum and may get them focused on something other than "old age" and their elderly counterparts.

Ask your children to participate in the caregiving process with you. Their presence in the life of an aged parent or loved one can dispel boredom with shining moments of genuine spontaneity and happiness.

A *pet* may also have an amazing effect on your parent, allowing her to take responsibility for an animal that loves her unconditionally. If she can walk a dog every day, the exercise will be a bonus to the entire relationship, as well as stimulate socialization. The positive effect of animals on the elderly has been substantiated so thoroughly that federal law requires operators of subsidized housing to allow their elderly tenants to keep pets.

If your parent is not up to the effort of a dog or cat, perhaps a smaller animal, such as a bird or a fish or hamster, can provide the desired companionship. If your loved one does not want to take on this responsibility, then bring your dog along for visits. You will be surprised at the positive reaction your pet will provide.

Conflicting Generational Needs

As a member of the sandwich generation, you likely will find times when the needs of the younger and the older generation conflict with each other. Discuss with your family your role as caregiver *before* it becomes a reality, to prepare members of both generations for what is coming. It is perfectly natural to think first of the needs of your family, but whenever possible try to include your children and spouse in the caregiving experience. The kids can visit their grandmother while you attend to her monthly bills, and your spouse can become involved in some of the heavy lifting, such as shopping for groceries and household repairs. Remember to always thank your spouse and children for their participation in caregiving.

Elder Love Life

Yes, there is *dating* and *sex* after age sixty-five. This truth may be one of the best kept secrets in human history, and you may find yourself uncomfortably confronted by it in the course of your caregiving. It can be awkward to watch your eighty-year-old mother gaze wistfully into the eyes of a gentleman five years her senior, but the fact is that for most human beings, it is never too late to fall in love. The feeling remains one of life's greatest ones, a sense of being alive, as they say — *really alive.*

In old age, the emotional and psychological aspects of the sexual experience take on more importance than they have in our youth. At the same time, you should remember that sex is very good exercise. The National Institute on Aging has a brief pamphlet addressing sexuality in later life, and there is even a small body of literature on the subject. If the idea really bothers you, think of it not as *sex* but as *dating.*

Falls in the Home

Your parent in old age will also face, on a daily basis, a number of more serious risks to her health. Foremost among them are *falls* in the home. As we have observed, problems with balance and the failure to use walkers or canes, as well as clutter, can all contribute to what can be a crippling experience, even a potentially fatal one. The best response to the problem of falls is to review and implement the safety precautions described earlier in Chapter 5 / Step 3. Exercises can also help improve balance while maintaining flexibility and strength. Encourage your parent to move around as much as possible. She might want to take up *tai chi*, an ancient Chinese art that cultivates controlled movements.

Osteoporosis and Arthritis

Osteoporosis and *arthritis* are two conditions that we characteristically associate with old age. The former disease causes bones to lose their hardness and density, becoming very brittle and breaking easily. The loss of density can result as well in compression fractures in the vertebrae.

Unfortunately, prevention of osteoporosis must begin early, with lots of exercise and a diet with plenty of calcium and vitamin D; but such a diet at any time of life will decrease the rate of bone loss, while reducing fractures by one-third.

Ideally an elderly person needs 1,200mg of calcium daily, along with 400 international units of vitamin D. To consume this much, an adult would have to drink a quart of milk daily, at a minimum. A calcium supplement with vitamin D added satisfies the requirement more easily.

Responding to Osteoporosis

A parent suffering from osteoporosis should remain as active as possible, which may be a daunting task, since persons afraid of falling tend to remain sedentary. However, exercises such as walking and swimming, or even riding a stationary bicycle, will strengthen muscles and help bones to grow thicker and stronger. Such efforts also improve balance, coordination, and reflexes, all of which lessens the chance of falling.

Drug therapy is also available for osteoporosis, with new treatments emerging constantly. Bisphosphonates have reduced fractures in postmenopausal women by as much as 50 percent. These include Fosamax (alendronate) and Actonel (risedronate), which increase density of the bone and slow its loss.

Evista (raloxifene) strengths bone just as estrogen does, but without the side-effects of breast tenderness and vaginal bleeding. Estrogen for osteoporosis, not often recommended for men, is effective, but also is associated with breast cancer, heart disease, and stroke. Your mother should consult her PCP or a specialist in deciding on this therapy.

Certain drugs that may have been prescribed for your elderly parent can cause bone loss as a side effect. An example is glucocorticoid steroids, sometimes found in medicines for asthma, arthritis, insomnia, and seizures. Consult your parent's physician concerning these and other medicines your parent may be taking.

Kinds of Arthritis

Arthritis is actually a family of more than a hundred diseases causing joint pain, stiffness, and swelling. Rheumatoid arthritis is an autoimmune disease, and osteoarthritis is a degenerative condition that destroys cartilage and joints. Gout and pseudogout are excruciatingly painful forms of arthritis. Gout occurs when an excess of uric acid collects and forms sharp crystals in the joints. In pseudogout excess calcium pyrophosphate collects at the larger joints, such as the hip, shoulder, or knee. Since there is no cure for arthritis, therapy aims at maximum symptomatic relief.

The warning signs of arthritis are familiar to most of us: swelling, inflammation and pain at the joints, stiffness, especially upon rising in the morning, and restricted movement. Nonmedical treatments include warm baths and heating pads to relieve pain, as well as cold packs to reduce swelling and lessen pain. Massage can also help.

When not actively suffering an attack, your parent should exercise to keep joints limber and freely moving. Exercise also increases her range of movement and relieves pain and inflammation. Again, *tai chi* may be useful.

Aids to getting around with arthritis include canes, walkers, and splints. Shock-absorbing insoles in shoes will relieve pain. Devices such as jar openers and faucet grippers can ease certain tasks for people with arthritis.

Medicating Arthritis

Drug therapies are also available, including aspirin, acetaminophen, and ibuprofen are widely prescribed to relieve pain. Acetaminophen has the fewest side effects. So-called NSAIDs (non-steroidal anti-inflammatory drugs) are also effective, but can result in unpleasant side effects such as ulcers, vomiting, and water retention.

Rheumatoid arthritis responds well to DMARDs (disease-modifying antirheumatic drugs), especially at the onset of the disease. More traditional therapies include gold shots and penicillamine, and are used when patients cannot tolerate more modern drugs, though these can take two to six months to have an effect.

NSAIDs and colchicine are used to treat gout and pseudogout.

Stomach Troubles

Digestive disorders include ulcers, gas, and heartburn, hemorrhoids, diverticular disease, and difficulty swallowing, as well as constipation and diarrhea.

Diet bears directly on gas, heartburn, and ulcers, and tobacco and alcohol only aggravate matters. Gas is normal, though sometimes embarrassing. Foods high in fiber, low in fat, are generally regarded among the healthiest things we can eat, but also cause gas — included here are beans, legumes, broccoli, brussel sprouts, cauliflower, raisins, bran. It is best to retain these foods in the diet, but cut down on their quantities to reduce gas.

Your parent simply should avoid any foods that cause heartburn, as well as eating meals that are smaller and more frequent. She should not eat at bedtime, and should sleep with her head elevated.

Persistent indigestion, as opposed to the kind caused by Christmas turkey, may indicate a disorder of the digestive tract, such as ulcers. Most ulcers are caused by a bacteria called H. pylori, which destroys the layer of mucous that coat the walls of the stomach. They may also be caused or aggravated by long term use of aspirin and NSAIDs. Smoking, caffeine, and alcohol should be avoided. Ulcers may cause internal bleeding or contribute to a blockage of the intestine, so your parent should consult his doctor if he has any of the symptoms associated with ulcers, such as a burning sensation in his stomach, bloating, and nausea after eating.

Hemorrhoids

Hemorrhoids are small, painful protuberances formed by excessive straining of the muscles around the anus. They may also bleed. It takes time and a change in diet — to fibers and fluids — to address the issue.

Not all rectal bleeding is caused by hemorrhoids, however, and your parent should see his doctor whenever it occurs.

Diverticulosis and Diverticulitis

Diverticulosis, the presence of small sacs developing in the lining of the intestine, is quite common among the elderly, and is treated mainly with rest and a high-fiber diet.

Diverticulitis is a more serious condition which causes the sacs to become inflamed, leading to more inflammation or a perforation of the intestine wall. The response includes antibiotics, IV fluids, and surgery.

Dysphagia

If your parent has *difficulty swallowing,* or *dysphagia,* consult a doctor. Causes include dry mouth, weakened throat muscles, or more serious conditions including cancer and stroke. Difficulty in swallowing may interfere with eating and lead to malnutrition, among other things.

Heart Failure

Heart failure is common among the elderly. As we age, the heart muscle weakens and pumps blood with less efficiency, causing blood to back up in one of the heart's chambers. Other symptoms include fluid retention, shortened breath, and fatigue. The reduced blood flow causes the body to produce more blood in compensation. This excess only aggravates the situation, leading to a worse backlog of blood in the heart, and increasing congestive heart failure.

This progressive condition can be controlled, though not cured. Therapy involves medicines that regulate the heart rate and diuretics that reduce the excess fluid. A diet low in salt usually accompanies these other treatments. On occasion, a pacemaker or defibrillator is prescribed or installed. Over the last 20 years there have been huge progressive strides in the care of heart-related issues. Pay careful attention to your loved one(s) aches and pains, and if appropriate, consult a cardiologist for a complete check-up.

The Loss of Cognitive Abilities

Among the most traumatic of all things affecting aging parents is *the loss of cognitive abilities.* This consequence of aging is more significant than a little forgetfulness. As many as half the people aged sixty-five or older report difficulties remembering things. Such is "age-related memory loss," and it is the norm. This can be a scary time for your parent, so try to be as understanding as possible and repeat things several times if necessary, without judgment.

However, approximately 40 percent of older adults experiencing memory loss will develop dementia, Alzheimer's, or some other form of substantial cognitive impairment.

Dementia

Dementia is a family of symptoms rooted in a number of causes. Symptoms include extreme memory loss, confusion, disorientation, changes of personality, and difficulties with math and language. Dementia, in turn, results from some other predisposing condition or disease. Approximately 10 percent of people over sixty-five experience dementia, as do nearly half of those older than eighty-five.

The symptoms of dementia yield a diagnosis of Alzheimer's in about 60 percent of all cases. Another 30 percent, known as multi-infarct dementia, are rooted in strokes so minor that the patient often does not notice them. The remaining cases result from various causes, such as AIDS, Huntington's disease, Parkinson's, or long-term alcoholism.

The early symptoms are difficult to distinguish from ordinary memory loss. Sooner or later, though, dementia will being to disrupt your parent's life, and yours as well. The memory loss becomes problematic. Your father cannot remember where he put his glasses, and he has worn them since the second grade. Attempting to understand why he cannot locate them, he concludes that someone is "playing a trick" on him. Thus, a family disruption occurs.

What Is Happening?

Such is not the case with normal memory loss. How can you determine what is happening?

Approaching the issue is a big step, and should be done delicately and with tact. When the right moment presents itself you might bring up the subject – and you may start by relating your own forgetfulness, and proceed from there.

If your father refuses to consider the possibility of a significant loss of his cognitive abilities, make your own appointment with his doctor. A social worker may be useful, and you should also consult the Alzheimer's association in your area. This can be located online by going to the Alzheimer's Association website at www.alz.org and clicking on the "In My Area" option, or by calling (800) 272-3900.

An examination by your parent's PCP should yield an initial diagnosis of some sort, either probable dementia or some physical (and possible treatable) condition.

A Complete Evaluation

A complete evaluation of your parent may be performed by his PCP or a specialist. This exam begins with a review of his medical history and a review of his overall demeanor and mental state. The doctor may administer a Mini-Mental State Examination (MMSE), a brief which determines your father's skill with simple tasks, his ability to recall new information, and to calculate and think abstractly.

Blood and urine samples will be checked for possible physical causes of your parent's confused condition, and a neurological exam will test his reflexes, sensory function, and coordination. A psychiatric review will eliminate such causes as depression. Imaging techniques such as CT and MRI will detect whether any damage to the brain has occurred. A spinal tap will be done to determine the presence of any disease of the nervous system.

The diagnosis of dementia proceeds by this process of eliminating other causes, an approach that yields correct diagnoses 95 percent of the time.

Alzheimer's Disease

Alzheimer's disease will be diagnosed in 60 percent of patients tested. Alzheimer's results from the physical degeneration of brain cells into *plaques* and *tangles* — clumps of abnormal protein formed in the midst of damaged or dead tissue, and bundles of fibers within brain cells. The causes of Alzheimer's are not yet known. In fact, Alzheimer's, like dementia, may not be a single disease but a family of related conditions.

Multi-infarct Dementia

Multi-infarct dementia is diagnosed in 30 to 40 percent of cases. This disorder is rooted in tiny strokes, often unnoticed by the patient, that disrupt the flow of blood to the brain, with subsequent death of tissue.

The results of the test may be shared by the doctor with your father and, often, the entire family. If you have reason to suspect that your parent does not want to know what the diagnosis is, ask him.

When Dementia Is Confirmed

Once the diagnosis is known, assure your parent that he will not be alone. Nor will you — you cannot afford to be. You must deal with the same kind of sadness, fear, and uncertainty that will plague the patient. A grieving process will begin for you, and for the family. Do not resist it, but let it unfold at its own pace.

Begin to seek the help and assistance you will need. This search begins with another trip to the Alzheimer's Association website mentioned above. The Association has local chapters all around the country, which can assist you in finding the support you will need.

Your parent is going to decline into a condition in which he cannot make his own decisions. With this inevitability in mind, he should appoint a durable power of attorney, draft a last will and testament, and resolve and sign all advance directives. (These are discussed in detail in Chapter 6 / Step 4, above.) Having a health-care proxy will be critical sooner or later.

Consideration should be given to the issue of how your parent's care will be paid for and to the matter of his living situation. The latter may involve skilled nursing home care.

Appreciate the time that your parent remains somewhat lucid and accessible to you and other family members. Talk with him about what he wants done, and ask especially if there is some matter he feels a need to address while still marginally functional.

Simplify, Simplify

Treatment for a case of dementia begins with the simplification of the parent's everyday life to a calm and orderly routine — something that he can depend on. The planning should be flexible enough to deal with the daily changes that can characterize the progress of dementia. Remember that environment is a great influence on mood and disposition, and respond accordingly.

Medicating Dementia

Medications for dementia may temporarily reverse the symptoms in some patients, but there is no cure as yet. Treatment for multi-infarct dementia addresses the strokes that cause it. Some cases of Alzheimer's are treated with medicines that stop or slow the breakdown of acetylcholine in the patient's brain. Acetylcholine affects a person's capacity for memory and coherent thought. A different therapy concentrates on another chemical in the brain, glutamate.

Other than these, therapies for Alzheimer's address and ease the disease's symptoms — fear, violence and aggression, depression, agitation, insomnia, and delusions and hallucinations. These medicines are regarded as a last line of defense, because they do little besides sedate your parent, may contribute to further confusion on his part, and may have other side effects that only complicate his situation.

All the care issues discussed in the preceding chapters take on a new simplicity in cases of dementia. Try to break down all tasks into simple single-action steps. Don't just refer to "washing your hair," but begin with "wet your hair," and proceed from there in a stepwise fashion.

Coping with the Stress of Dementia

Cultivate calm and patience if you expect to get through this caregiving experience in one piece. Relaxation techniques, deep breathing, going for walks — all these activities have a calming and restorative affect that you will need repeatedly. Resort to a list of friends or support-group acquaintances when necessary, to sort out feelings and express frustrations and anger.

Above all, remember that you are not the target of your parent's dementia — he is. It's not about you. It's a disease. In your parent's world, logic and proportion are things of the past, and he has lost his capacity to understand and explain what is happening to him. The temptation to take all this personally will be overwhelming, and, in fact, you will not always be able to resist it. Nevertheless, the chaos and confusion that dementia brings to the lives of all it touches are not the result of your parent's conscious will, but of the disease, and the disease *only*.

You will need to simplify your parent's world, which will mean simplifying a bit of your own. Reduce all clutter. Position furniture where it is most accessible, and once in position, do not move it. Reduce noise to a minimum. Make signs to aid your parent, that is, label things: the door to the bathroom, the drawers of his dresser, and so on. Make decisions simple: do not ask what he wants for dinner, but offer a choice between chicken and fish. (If necessary, decide for him.) Above reduce all change to the most minimal level necessary.

Pay particular attention to things in the environment that underlie any of your parent's agitation, distress, and acting out. Look at the situation with detachment, with an eye to what might be upsetting him, rather than focusing on your loved one. Change the room, because you cannot change dementia.

Let your parent do, for himself and others, as much as possible. Encourage him to assist with simple household chores like mixing the frozen orange juice or bringing in the daily mail. See that he gets as much exercise as he can handle — a simple walk once a day, for instance. Play soft music or ambient-sound recordings. If he wants, get him a pet.

An Invincible Summer

Finally, give yourself, and those who assist you, credit for doing one of the most difficult tasks life can offer. You will probably think in terms of what more your could do, but an honest assessment of the work actually done needs to be made periodically, to maintain self-esteem and avoid the pitfalls of overwork and depression.

You may find that, viewed as objectively as possible, you and your helpers are doing an amazing job on terms that strain the bounds of possibility. The care of a parent suffering from dementia will call forth your deepest strengths, even as it taxes them more sorely than ever before. This time will be one of trial, but also one of discovery. In the words of Albert Camus: "In the midst of winter, I found within me an invincible summer."

The Risk of Depression

The onset of age begins a season of loss, and when loss occurs, we grieve. But as a caregiver, you need to recognize that *depression* is not grief. Apathy is not mourning. Malaise is not ordinary sadness. Depression is an illness caused by irregularities in brain chemistry, and it is treatable, though it often requires the intervention of a physician. Contributing factors include stress, loneliness, boredom, and the influence of other physical illnesses. Signs of trouble can include:

- Sadness without any discernible cause.
- Changes in eating or weight without noticeable cause.
- Insomnia or other changes in sleeping habits.
- Feelings of worthlessness, of hopelessness.
- Lack of interest in grooming, appearance, and hygiene.
- Loss of interest in favorite things, hobbies, activities, people.
- Spontaneous crying, without apparent cause.
- Increased drinking of alcohol or use of tobacco.
- Expressions of suicidal ideation.

The appearance of these symptoms should get your attention. Their persistence for more than a week should prompt medical action – an evaluation for depression by a clinician and, if deemed necessary, treatment with a variety of psychiatric tools. Any talk of suicide is abnormal, and if your loved one has a plan for hurting himself, immediate intervention is necessary.

Further, depression also leaves your loved one in a weakened condition, prone to other illnesses as well.

We are often taught that depression – obsessive, compulsive thoughts of suicide – is simply self-pity, or some other form of character failing, and if your loved one suffers from this misconception, he probably will resist getting help. For your own peace of mind, you should insist that he be tested by a trained clinician.

I remember when my own parents were in their mid-70s, I would ask them how they were doing, and they would reply, "falling apart." They seemed to have endless trips to the doctor, constant ailments, and an overriding sadness where their future was heading. They were concerned that each day they were losing more of "the way things used to be." Our job as caregivers is to stay positive, maintain a sense of humor, be kind and thoughtful, and try to be as understanding as possible. That is the best that we can do.

Responding to Elder Abuse

It's depressing to even think we have to discuss this subject, but *elder abuse* is quite apparent in our society and can take on many forms, including physical, emotional, and verbal. There is also financial abuse, such as theft, and general neglect.

In Others

If your loved one is in a nursing home or other facility, you should be alert to things like unexplained bruises. Even if he is suffering from some form of dementia, be sure that his fears and anxieties do not have any basis in reality.

Insult and isolation – leaving your parent or loved one alone for extended periods of time – are also forms of abuse. Any time that your loved one is restrained, you should demand an explanation. If she appears to be groggy and over-medicated, ask why.

Neglect may take the form of ignoring a patient's call bell, or failing to reposition him regularly in his bed, but these may be more sins of omission than commission. Abuse is intentional.

Report all signs of abuse immediately – do not wait for another incident to occur.

And in Yourself

Saddest of all is the situation in which the home caregiver, who performs a terrifically hard job and only intends the best, is pushed by circumstances beyond her own limit and lashes out at the loved one in her care. If you find yourself edging toward such a risk, get help as soon as you can. Get some help with the caregiving, to begin with, from a spouse, from your children if possible, or even from a hired professional. Help may be found online at the National Center on Elder Abuse(www.ncea.aoa.gov), which has a particularly useful page on Caregiver Supports at www.ncea.aoa.gov/ncearoot/Main_Site/Find_Help/Resources/Caregiver_Support.aspx. Another source of support is the Family Caregiver Alliance, www.caregiver.org/caregiver/jsp/home.jsp, which hosts a Caregiver Online Group (www.caregiver.org/caregiver/jsp/content_node.jsp?nodeid=3 47) that offers a forum for the discussion of the stresses and challenges of home caregiving.

CHAPTER 10 / STEP 8

Create a support team

What kind of help can a caregiver expect to find, and how can she best care for herself over the long journey of caring for an aging parent?

Asking for Help

As you may have noticed, availing yourself of the help of friends, neighbors, and family members has been a continuing theme throughout these Steps. Most people are more than likely to offer their assistance, they just don't know what to do. Find your volunteers a job to do – anything that will lighten your load – and remember to reward them. Also, do not be discouraged by the occasional refusal, and do not take these personally. We all have our own lives and our own limits. Be sure to thank those who do participate with you in the caregiving, and do not wait until the very end to do so. Thoughtful gifts may be appropriate at any time for actions taken in these circumstances.

The National Family Caregiver Support Program

Don't neglect the community in which you live. The Older Americans Act created the Administration on Aging in 1965 and funded the establishment of an Area Agency on Aging (AAoA) in each state. Subsequent legislation in 2000 reauthorized the Act and created the National Family Caregiver Support Program (NFCSP). Grants are given to each state, based on the share of its population aged 70 and older, to fund and administer at the state level a range of services that assist family and informal caregivers with the care of their elderly loved ones at home for as long as possible.

Families are the major provider of long-term care, but caregiving exacts a heavy emotional, physical, and financial toll. Twenty-two percent of caregivers are caring for two individuals, and 8 percent are caring for three or more. Almost half of these caregivers are over the age of 50, and one-third of these rate their own health as fair-to-poor.

The Program provides five types of service:

- information on services available;
- assistance in gaining access to services;
- individual counseling, organization of support groups, and training for caregivers;
- respite care;
- supplemental services on a limited basis.

The NFCSP works in conjunction with other state and community-based services to produce coordinated support for caregivers. Initial studies have shown that these services reduce the levels of depression, anxiety, and stress among caregivers, enabling them to provide care for longer periods and thus avoiding or delaying the need for more costly institutional care.

Grandparents and relatives other than parents over the age of 55 who are caring for grandchildren younger than 18 may also participate in the program. These same two groups may also participate if they provide care for disabled adults aged 18 to 59.

In fiscal year 2011, the NFCSP received funding totaling $153.9 million.

Use the Area Agency on Aging

Your state Area Agency on Aging (AAoA) may be located by accessing the Eldercare Locator at eldercare.gov/Eldercare.NET/Public/Index.aspx, where you may search by Zip code, city and state, or by topic of interest, from Alzheimer's Disease to Volunteerism.

Before you call your AAoA, make a list of your parent's needs and concerns, and rank these in order of importance. Then, when you make contact with the AAoA, address these issues in order and take careful notes.

Gather as much information as you can from as many sources as you can find, and keep it organized. (If organization is not your long suit, ask a friend or family member to help.) Carry a small notebook with you, and keep another beside the phone and the computer, so that information is not stored on scraps of paper and empty matchbooks. Try to keep your notes dated, and try also to get the names of the individuals with whom you speak.

The Long-Term Care Ombudsman

Each state also has an long-term care ombudsman who advocates for the residents of nursing homes and for their families. The ombudsman is knowledgeable about the nursing home facilities in your state and can assist you with references and with the resolution of problems in a facility. Some ombudsmen function at the local level as well.

Aid from Charities and Employers

Charities such as the United Way can greatly assist the family caregiver, as can churches, mosques, and synagogues. Examples include Jewish Family Services, Catholic Charities, and, in Chicago, the recently-founded Senior Muslim Care (temp.seniormuslimcareorg.officelive.com/default.aspx).

Your employer and that of your spouse may also contribute to the caregiving effort in the form of time off authorized under the Family and Medical Leave Act (FMLA). If your company has more than 50 employees and you have spent more than 1,250 hours working over the last 12 months, you may be eligible for up to 12 weeks of paid leave to provide care for a family member. A few states have their own equivalents of the Act, and your company's health insurance may also offer support to the employee who doubles as a caregiver.

Spread the Word

Communicate with all concerned with your parent's care — family members, friends, peers, and professionals — and document everything that you do. If you take Mom out to the California Pizza Kitchen, take your digital camera along and email photos of the event to the rest of the team. Not only is it fun to document the event, but it will give the parent and family members something to talk about. Phone calls and letters are encouraged too.

Hiring Outside Help

You may need to hire outside assistance, such as a geriatric case manager, or, around the home, a driver to chauffeur Mom around, a cook to prepare meals, or a general maid and housekeeper. Consider local colleges for students willing to work in exchange for money or room and board. Remember to ask for references and, if possible, conduct a background check. Always pay by check, and do not let your aged parent tip the help with cash. A professional accountant can advise you concerning the fine points of the economics of hired health-care assistants. And if you're admitting strangers to you house or your parent's, don't neglect to secure all of your valuables in out-the-way places.

Caring for Caregivers

Finally, *care for yourself.* Create a support team for you. As the primary caregiver for your parent, your health and well-being are to be highly valued, though in fact it is the one area most caregivers neglect.

Reach out to other people, your friends and neighbors, anyone who is in the same situation you are. If you belong to a church, learn what help it has to offer and use it. Check out local civic groups as well, such as the Rotary and Civitan International. If you or your loved one is a veteran of the armed forces, contact your local office of Veterans Affairs and ask what assistance is available.

One the Web, the U.S. Administration on Aging has a page (http://www.aoa.gov/AoARoot/AoA_Programs/Tools_ Resources/national_organizations.aspx) that links to support groups in the following categories: Comprehensive National Organizations, Alzheimer's Disease, Elder Rights, Faith-Based, Family Caregiving, Homelessness, Housing, In-Home and Long-Term Care, Minority Organizations, Nutrition, Research and Education, and Transportation. The Family Caregiver Alliance website (www.caregiver.org/caregiver/ jsp/home.jsp) devotes a lengthy and detailed page to the subject of self-care for the caregiver at www.caregiver.org/ caregiver/jsp/content_node.jsp?nodeid=847.

On-the-Job Burnout

Don't forget that caregiving is a job, and that every worker needs some time off on a regular basis. Beware of overwork, and watch for the signs of burnout:

- lack of energy
- over susceptibility to colds and minor illnesses
- feeling exhausted all the time, even when you awaken in the morning after a night's sleep
- neglect of your own needs, because you're too busy or you have stopped caring
- lack of any satisfaction with the caregiving experience
- inability to relax
- increasingly irritable and impatient, especially with the loved one for whom you care
- feelings of helplessness and hopelessness
- inability to sleep.

Learn to set limits on what you can do, and overcome any reluctance your may have to ask for help. When people offer to help, always say yes, yes, and *yes!* Let them know what specific help you need and then, let them have at it! I asked one of my friends if she could stop by now and then to bring my dad some of his favorite juice, which they had shared together on one occasion. She took it on herself to stop by weekly with two bottles of juice and sugar-free cookies. Margot loved being helpful, and my dad enjoyed the company and thoughtfulness. Her kindness was so appreciated and was such a great help to me during the caregiving experience. He looked forward to her visits, and I looked forward to the break.

Realities of Caregiving

Examine your motives. Are you caregiving to resolve old guilts? Do you feel compelled to provide care? What drives your actions? As much as possible, the decision to provide care for an aging parent should be a conscious choice on your part, not a compelling need rooted in ancient family history and prior difficulties.

Identify your parent's real needs, and separate the truly essential from the mere nice touches. Ask for your parent's ideas on her care. Put it all in writing and decide what is necessary, what might be done, and what can be eliminated.

Keep an eye on yourself. Don't run away with caregiving, but maintain a realistic perspective on the actual needs of the situation from day to day. What is truly pressing and demands your personal attention now? You need not jeopardize your own health or career, nor should you neglect your own children to care for your mother. Decide, on a daily basis, which of her needs are most important — the things that only you can take care of — and plan your day around those needs. Plan conservatively, for it is easier to expand your to-do list than to trim it down.

Even with this kind of planning, you will have to learn how to say *no* to your parent. Just as important, learn to say *no* to yourself. Do not undertake caregiving to satisfy feelings of guilt or inadequacy. Look at your mother's needs and your own motives as clinically as possible. Then decide what to do and what to pass over.

It is even harder when you don't live near your parent(s). I remember feeling so guilty not being right by my mother's side when she was ill. But I lived in Atlanta and she was in Michigan. The best I could do was to get on a plane when totally necessary. Or, even seeing my dad more often, I always felt "I could do a better job than anyone else" so I needed to be there as much as possible. These feelings are all very real, but the reality is, you can't do it all, all the time. So give yourself a break.

Emotional Pitfalls

Try to avoid the emotional pitfalls of feelings like guilt and helplessness, personal demons that you will have to confront more than once during your caregiving experience. Consider not only what you feel you are neglecting but also, as objectively as possible, note the good work you are doing. If necessary, make a list to remind yourself of all you do.

Anger and resentment can ruin a day or a week. Instead of focusing on what others, including your parent, are not doing, ask what you can do to change the situation for the better. If resentment is a problem, back off for a while, and do less. Give yourself a break and try to relax. Ask your spouse to assist, and, of course, listen to his thoughts on the matter of your parent's care. Analyze your anger. Write down its causes, and ask what it is within you that is affected so adversely by them. Then ask how you can address these personal needs of your own. You can change and grow through these emotions instead of being swept away by them.

Grief Heals

Finally, let yourself grieve. Let yourself feel the very real sorrow of this time in your life and the life of your parent. Take time off from work and social obligations to spend some time alone or to talk over your feelings with your spouse or a close friend, a clergyman or even a therapist. Avail yourself of caregiver support groups and networks to dispel the notion that you are alone with your responsibilities. Your AAoA can help you find such organizations, and you may also contact

Children of Aging Parents at (800) 227-7294 or on the Web at www.caps4caregivers.org. The National Self-Help Clearing-house is another such resource, available at (212) 817-1822 or www.selfhelpweb.org. More specific issues may be addressed with the aid of such groups and organizations as the American Cancer Society, the Alzheimer's Association, and Alcoholics Anonymous.

Above all, learn as much as you can about the very real work of caregiving. You can learn this on your own and from other caregivers in your area. If you have educated yourself about what to expect, you can prepare accordingly. I know that if I had had a book such as this one before I started on my path of caregiving, I would have done a much better job, if only for a better understanding of what lay ahead.

CHAPTER 11 / STEP 9

Embrace this time

Collecting Recollections

When I think about the final months I spent with my mom and dad, I recall many talks of the past, uncovering forgotten memories, a feeling of life well accomplished and the moments of just living life in the present. I call this time creating a "Treasure Box" of memories. It is all about embracing this time as a caregiver with your loved one(s).

When you imagine a treasure box, you may be filled with anticipation and wonder what might be inside. You might open one and find some real jewels or just some old papers seemingly not worth keeping. You might sort through your finds and ponder what to do with what you have discovered – should you share your secrets, or hide them. And when the box is empty, all is gone, nothing is left.

At this incredibly valuable time in your loved one(s) life, they *are* the Treasure Box. Taking the time to uncover all their treasures will not only be a gift that they will enjoy giving, but one more valuable to you than you may have ever imagined. It can actually be an incredibly rewarding time to embrace the stories, examine the photographs, listen to certain music, enjoy special foods, revisit memorable places, and sometimes, just be still and listen to the "quiet noises."

Listening, watching, talking, walking, dancing, singing, reading, visiting, are all part of the process of uncovering the many days of long past, the thoughts of the day as well as their cares and fears of the future.

I remember one day, my mom and I went out to lunch, and were so engrossed in our conversation that the café staff began setting the tables for dinner when we finally left! Hours and hours of triumphs and sadness and joy and tears and wonder filled her treasure box until we could not eat another piece of lemon meringue pie. I will never forget that day, ever.

Another time, when my dad was in an assisted living home, I found one of his favorite polka CDs. One of his Italian caregivers, who barely spoke English, came in to find me playing the music at top volume and singing with my dad. Well, he joined in with us, and we danced and cried as we saw my dad so full of joy, singing away, recalling his favorite songs of long ago. He knew every word to every song! Just a simple day, but filled with the most sincere of emotions.

Physically, you can get a box and begin to assemble the "treasures of their lives" . . . while they are alive! You can add photographs, records, special menus or baseball cards, even hats, awards, pressed flowers, or special poems, cards and books to a keepsake that you can talk about together. Share it with other family members, or keep some feelings to yourself, but do it! Have your mom or dad record sayings, songs, or messages, keep a journal, record video conversations, have them write down their thoughts. Ask them to tell you about each "jewel" in their box, so you can better understand their lives as they were actually lived.

Without a physical box, you can also create their emotional treasure box in your heart. Thoughts of children, pets, playing games, puzzles, walks in the garden, watching old movies, even a piece of clothing – all this and more can bring an array of memories and feelings flooding to the surface. Provide activities that will stimulate your loved one's recollections: an outing to a baseball game or concert, or to a local church or festival, even to an ethnic restaurant.

Now that the box is open, what might you expect? Sometimes feelings of laughter, sadness, joy, tenderness, frustration, and even disappointment may occur – the spectrum of human emotions from one end to the other. It is their life story, and they know it is coming to an end. Embrace these moments, seek understanding, gain wisdom, and appreciate the gifts you receive and those you are able to give. When you look back at this time, my hope for you is that, going forward, you will live and love life differently now, with new meaning and with gratitude. Your box will never be empty.

CHAPTER 12 / STEP 10

Prepare for death and dying

What can a caregiver expect to encounter during the dying process, death itself, and in the grief that follows?

The Process of Ending

Death is not just a single event, but a process, and usually the process begins with denial. Death is located in the future, not the present. It will happen later, some other time, not now. But eventually and inevitably *now* comes to the present.

Dying is part of life, and we all are destined to experience it, at some point or another. As denial gives way to reality, you may avail yourself of the time that is left by serving your dying parent in her final days, expressing love and devotion, resolving unfinished issues, recalling the shining moments of her life, promises for your future, and, finally, in saying goodbye.

The Legalities of Death

First, attend to the legalities of the situation. If your parent has made no will, designated no health-care proxy or durable power of attorney, or filed no advance directives, now is the time to do so. If these legal steps are not taken, you run the risk of having your mother die in an intensive care unit, the object of heroic measures of treatment that she would not have wanted.

If these legal documents exist, locate them and keep them on hand. Copy any directives she may have filed and pass them on to her doctor. If they do not exist, try to have them prepared as efficiently as possible. But remember that these documents can only be prepared while your parent is mentally competent. If this is not the case, you may find yourself in court, petitioning for the right to make your parent's decisions for her, a process that can be complicated if other parties, such as your siblings, have differing ideas about how your parent's case should be handled.

The Ongoing Conversation Continues

Assuming all legalities are addressed, sit and talk things over with your parent. Her doctor can give both of you some idea of what the coming days will bring. Find out her own thoughts on the process.

If your parent is unable to participate in such conversations, you will still want to go over the situation and discuss the concerns of everyone in the family at some length. No one should put the emotions on hold during this time, but should freely express their own individual response to the impending death of their parent or grandparent or loved one.

Everyone should be prepared to implement their parent's will regarding issues faced at the end of life. Advance directives take on enormous significance at this point, and caregivers need to reconcile themselves with actually having to enforced their mother's or father's last wishes regarding treatment.

If your mother has directed that she not be resuscitated or placed on a ventilator, you need to be certain that you can say *no* to these treatment options should the time come.

Be wary of lying to your parent about her diagnosis and prognosis. Such deception can result in unwanted treatments and a protracted and painful death. Tact and gentleness have major roles to play in this kind of communication, but always tell your parent the truth. A sense of hope rooted in falsehood is a worse fate than despair.

Listen to Your Parent

Allow your parent to determine the course of ordinary conversations when you are with her. Avoid small talk, but remember that these conversations needn't be dramatic affairs. Listen to your mother if she wants to talk, and let her guide the discussion, allowing it to go wherever she needs it to go. Do not change the subject or disagree with what she says, no matter how "negative" you feel it may be. Do not try to "cheer her up." Instead, let her have the freedom to express herself as she really is, really feels, and really thinks. Remember that these conversations are among the last she will ever have.

She likely will find consolation in reflecting on her life, including her family life, and this sort of summing up is a good sign and necessary. Let her know how she has helped you through the years with your own life, and what her influence has meant to other people as well.

If, in the moment, you find yourself at a loss for words, *listen*. And if she does not wish to talk, let her have her way.

Respond to Your Parent's Point of View

Consider her point of view. We are often more afraid of the process of dying than of the death itself, and most of us fear the idea of dying in pain. If pain is a problem, discuss the matter with her physician and see what he can recommend in the way of medicine to relieve unnecessary suffering. You may want to consult a palliative care specialist, an expert on pain and its control. If so, ask your doctor for a referral.

Let her know that, at the end of life, she is not a burden to you and the family, or to anyone else. Also let her know that you and your family are all right, and will remain all right, though you will miss her presence in your lives and affairs.

Five Stages of Grief

As a guide for this final journey with your loved one, familiarize yourself with the five stages of grief as described by Elizabeth Kübler-Ross in her book, *On Death and Dying*, published in 1969 and based on interviews with 500 people in the last stages of their lives.

The five stages are *denial, anger, bargaining, depression,* and *acceptance.* Kübler-Ross noted that these stages may not occur in this order and that they probably will not be discrete and complete unto themselves. They will overlap, and sometimes you may seem to be repeating yourself emotionally. Such experiences are ordinary and to be expected. You will experience these emotions at the onset of the dying process and perhaps again, in the aftermath of death itself.

Denial

The defense mechanism of *denial* may be conscious or unconscious. Your parent may insist that she feels fine, or deny that the doctor's diagnosis is true. Do not argue with her. Instead, accept that her denial gives her room to move, a psychologically necessary avoidance of the fact of her own ending. Denial allows her take on the ultimate truth of her mortality one day at a time.

Be aware that you, and the others giving care to your parent, will pass through these same experiences. You will experience denial in some form as well, perhaps simply as a statement that the time of death has not yet actually come.

Anger

Anger is a common response to the fact of dying. Your mother's anger may be directed toward herself, for being ill, or toward those around her, who are unable to save her from death, or toward God in Heaven, for abandoning her to this fate. As with denial, allow your parent to have his own feelings at his own time. Do not argue with the unreasonableness of his anger, but accept that it is real, even predictable, and that he will simply go through it — feel it — as he dies. Should you become the focus of his anger, do not argue with him, but accept that this too will pass.

Bargaining

Anger tends to give way to *bargaining,* in which we attempt to make deals with God or the universe for a little more time alive in this world. *Let me recover,* we will offer, *and I will make amends to my children for the wrongs I have done them.* Bargaining can be about anything, from longer life itself to being allowed to live long enough to see the birth of a great-grandchild. These deals with fate tend to result in changes of behavior. Blasé denial and defiant anger yield to a vigorous interest in his health care.

If your parent has some realizable goal in mind for his survival, see what you and the family can do to bring it about. If he bargains with more general aspects of his life, like smoking cigarettes or being kinder to his grandchildren, encourage him. The bargaining is not likely to succeed, but it can give him a sense of participating in his own life.

Depression

When all the bargaining fails and the certainty of death is acknowledged, *depression* often results. Your parent may withdraw and turn away visitors and other company. His attitude will resemble that summed up in the depressive refrain, "What's the point?" Such feelings allow him to begin to disconnect from the things he loves in the world and the life around him. Again, do not attempt to "cheer him up." This sadness and depression are part of the grief that he can and must pass through.

Acceptance

Ideally, your parent will come to some degree of *acceptance* of his own death. This is the final stage of grief, often a sense of relief that all struggles are coming to a close. This time may be difficult to any caregiver who herself has yet to come to accept that the loss of her parent is inevitable. In this case, try to understand that your parent is moving to his own end in the best way possible for him.

Health Care at the End of Life

If possible, you may want your parent to pass away in the comfort of home or comfortable surroundings and the presence of his family. This sort of ending is desirable in many ways, but be aware that it entails strenuous effort on your part and the part of your family. This kind of death is home health care at its most intense and emotionally demanding.

Hospice Care

Your parent may opt for *hospice* care. The idea of hospice traces back to the 11th century. The medieval hospice, usually maintained by a monastic order, sheltered travelers and other pilgrims, as well as the destitute. Today, hospice refers to palliative care offered to the terminally ill, which can be extended in their own home or in a nursing facility or hospital. The modern concept sees death as a natural happening at the end of life rather than a medical battle calling for heroic measures. Hospice aims to enhance and enrich what life remains to your parent.

The first hospice in the United States was founded in New Haven, Connecticut in 1974. Today there are more than three thousand hospice programs in the U.S. Eighty percent of hospice care is provided in private homes and nursing homes.

Hospice aims to maintain the dignity of life while addressing any medical issues that impair the quality of your parent's existence. Recovery treatments and last-ditch lifesaving are not part of hospice care. Assuring your parent of a peaceful passing, and yourself a peaceful witness, are the goals in mind. No attempts are made to extend life; symptoms are treated to keep your parent comfortable. Hospice deals with the emotional, spiritual, and social effect of your parent's death.

Of course, your parent is free to leave hospice and return to hospital or in-home care at any time he desires.

The hospice team will include physicians and nurses, medical social workers and clergy, and, typically, a number of volunteers. You will plan and implement your parent's final care with these people. The plan will be reviewed from time to time, and updated as needed. The costs of hospice care are covered by Medicare and Medicaid, and by most private insurance.

I have visited several hospice facilities, and, remarkably, they are very warm and inviting, and seek first and foremost to meet the needs of the person facing death, while also catering to the needs of the grieving family. Some have comfortable television rooms, kitchens, and even outdoor exercise areas for family members to use. Sitting at one's bedside hour after hour, day after day, is not healthy for anyone. Therefore, these wonderful places take special pride in the care of the living and the dying.

Finding Hospice Care

To undertake hospice care, Medicare and other providers require a doctor's determination that your parent has less than six months to live. Should this not be the case, use the time to prepare for the eventuality of hospice. You will want to avoid any last-minute decisions on hospice care, which can result in a hurried, unpleasant experience for all concerned — symptomatic care is superficial and counseling services abbreviated and unsatisfying.

Programs may be found by contacting the National Hospice and Palliative Care Organization at (800) 658-9998 or on the Web at www.nhpco.org. Inquire concerning the hospice's certification and staffing, as well as admission requirements and credentials. If hospice will be hosted in your home, ask whether the service has an arrangement with a hospital or nursing home for in-home health care.

Should your parent need additional health care after entering hospice — say, for a broken limb incurred in a fall — that care will be provided as it would be if he were not in hospice. Should he decline to be treated, palliative care will take the place of regular therapy.

I believe that, wherever your loved one is when he/she finally passes on, the most important thing is to have a loving and caring environment of family members, children, and friends at their side. If at all possible, try to make that happen. When my mother passed away, all of her children and my dad, her husband of 50 years, were present. It was almost as if she waited to die until we were all close by. Then she closed her eyes and was gone.

Pain and Nutrition at the End of Life

What about issues of *pain* and *nutrition* in the final stage of life?

Pain and Pain Relief

Dying does not have to be painful, but should your parent need pain-relief, it will be available in hospice. This relief does not have to take the form of a sedative. Sometimes, patients experiencing the sort of extreme pain that interferes with sleep respond to painkillers with sedation. This effect is temporary, however, and in fact, necessary to allow your parent to make up for lost sleep. Once this balance is restored, the sedative effect wears off. If any remains it is probably caused by medications prescribed for anxiety or depression.

Morphine is usually given for severe pain management, and, once the suffering is under control, the dosage of the drug may be reduced. Addiction is not a risk if the drug is prescribed at the dosage levels appropriate to the relief of pain. When the pain is relieved, the dose is titrated downward in a way that results in none of the effects of opiate withdrawal. Pain relievers such as morphine can also boost your parent's mood, making it easier to breathe, relax, and sleep.

Above all, pain and suffering do not build character, and any other sort of symptomatic discomforts will also be addressed in hospice.

Nutrition

Concerning nutrition — the hydration of the dying parent or the insertion of feeding tubes — remember that as death approaches the body shuts down, dissipating the need for food and fluids. Force-feeding will only cause discomfort and pain.

Trajectories of Dying

What is your parent likely to experience in the course of his dying?

The sociologists Barney Glaser and Anselm Strauss developed the concept of patterns, or "trajectories," of death in the 1960s, publishing the results of their research of death in California hospitals in *Awareness of Dying* (1965). Like each life, each death is unique, but Glaser and Strauss determined four general, overall patterns that death can follow depending on its cause.

Sudden Death

First is *sudden death*, from accidents or violence, or from certain sudden health events such as heart attacks and strokes. This death is among the most shocking, because it is completely unexpected. Much regret and no small amount of guilt can be associated with a sudden death. The health care system, while it may respond effectively to the emergency, is not prepared to deal with you and your siblings' grief and need for counseling. Sudden death leaves many loose ends untied.

Cancer Deaths

Cancer deaths form a second trajectory, and probably the one that comes first to mind at the mention of death in a hospital. This pattern is one of continual descent, periodically leveling off in a plateau for some period of time. These plateaus parallel the application of various anti-cancer therapies, but once the treatments are exhausted, decline is steady and irreversible. This period allows family and friends to say their good-byes and tend to any matters left unfinished.

Chronic Illness

Chronic illness, the third pattern discerned by Glaser and Strauss, may be graphed as a series of peaks and valleys, sometimes seeming to approach the realm of recovery. The general trend of the patient's health, however, is one of decline. Congestive heart failure and chronic obstructive pulmonary disease (COPD) are examples of chronic illnesses that end in death. Such an up-and-down course can take as long as a year or more before the family and the patient finally give up on heroic measures and let nature take its course.

While your physician might not even recognize this trajectory as one leading to death, he will probably answer in the negative if you ask him whether your parent will survive for more than a year or so. If you and your parent find yourselves in the midst of a chronic illness, you may want to take hospice care into consideration.

A Long, Steady Decline

A long, steady decline is the fourth trajectory, usually experienced by people who have suffered from massive strokes or multiple heart attacks, a life-threatening microbial infection, or other catastrophic health events. At the end of the decline, there is no sign of improvement and no hope of recovery, and either your parent dies or decides — or you decide — to dispense with aggressive treatments and surrender to the inevitable. The question comes down to: how long will you continue to support life in such circumstances and conditions?

The Final Days

What can you, the caregiver, expect to see in the final stages of your parent's life?

Usually, death takes its own time, and you will witness its effects as it transpires. Your parent will become less mobile, and he usually becomes incontinent as well. As he eats and drinks less and less, he loses weight and grows thinner and thinner. His face becomes sunken and sallow. Wipe his mouth with a soft, damp cloth to assure that it is moist and fresh.

Your parent may have visions, hallucinate, or see old friends, including those who have preceded them in death. All of these phenomena are normal and no cause for alarm. Disturbing visions may be the result of bad dreams, and this situation can be addressed with adjustments to their medications.

Terminal Agitation

He may enter what is known as *terminal delirium* or *terminal agitation*, suddenly become confused, restless, and upset. This phenomenon usually results from the normal course of death as less and less oxygen reaches the brain, a situation complicated by pain relievers, dehydration, and changes in metabolism. The condition is not painful to your parent, but it may be very upsetting to you and other family and friends.

New-Found Energy

Sometimes the patient has new-found energy, and he tries to get out of bed, pulls out a catheter, or tussles with his caregiver with sudden overwhelming strength. Do not fight with him, but try, rather, to coax him back to bed and rest.

These symptoms usually occur very near the point of death. They may be aggravated if your parent believes he has some unfinished matter to which he must attend. Determine what this matter is and you will probably be able to urge him back to bed.

If medication has been prescribed for restlessness, the time has come to take it. Soft music may help calm him in his last moments, and you should speak to him in soft, gentle tones. Let him know who you are and that you are there with him, but do not be surprised or upset if he thinks you are someone else altogether. A massage, soft and gentle, may also have a calmative effect.

Concentrate on patience. Take a break when someone else can relieve you at the bedside. Terminal agitation may last for several hours, and transpire over the course of several days and nights.

Near death, your parent will begin to breathe differently, becoming shallow and quick or labored and difficult. He may experience Cheyne-Stokes respiration, with alternating periods of shallow and deep breathing. Breathing like this does no harm, though it may be troublesome to witness.

You may hear gurgling sounds from your parent's throat, the so-called "death rattle" caused by secretions he cannot cough up any longer. You may turn his head sideways to allow these fluids to drain. Wipe his mouth gently with a soft, moist sponge or cloth.

Notify the doctor or nurse of your parent's changes in breathing. You may elevate the head of his bed, and add another pillow to assist his breathing. Mouth breathing can dry the mouth, so moisten his lips and tongue with a wet cloth or chips of ice.

The Last Few Moments

In the final moments blood and oxygen become concentrated in the vital organs and leave the extremities of the body. Arms and legs will grow cool to the touch, and the lips and tip of the nose may turn a light bluish shade. Blood will begin to collect in the lower areas of the body, and you may notice tiny purplish blotches on the arms and legs.

Respond in a logical way to your parent's behavior at this point. If he kicks off the covers, he is probably overly warm. Cool him off with a damp cloth or ask a nurse for a fan to stir up the air in his room.

Hearing is the final sense to shut down. If you wish, continue to talk to your parent or even to read to him. A gentle touch is a comfort in these moments.

The Moment of Death

At the moment of death, some disturbing events may occur. Your parent may void his bowels and bladder. He may yell loudly or groan. These are the sounds of the last bit of air leaving his lungs, and no cause for alarm. Eyes and mouth may open at this time as well. Again, these are normal reflexes, and you should feel free to close his eyes and mouth.

You have no need to summon others immediately. Your parent's dying is over and no rush is needed. If you wish to sit quietly with him for a moment alone, do so. You may even bathe and groom him. Let other family know that death has come, and allow them their own time with their parent. Then it will be plenty of time to notify the doctor or nurse.

It seems that you are now emotionally exhausted and saddened by your loss, but now you have to move into a post-death gear to handle all the further arrangements.

After the Death

You will need to contact the mortuary and your clergyman if you wish. Do not let timing put you off — clergy would rather be notified in a timely manner in the middle of the night than to be summoned the next day, and the mortuary will simply wait until morning. Your parent's nurse will contact any companies that need to pick up rented hospital equipment, and she will also dispose of leftover medications.

Contact all members of your parent's immediate family, and, again, do not let matters of timing discourage you at this step. Family members usually prefer to know as soon as possible when death has occurred.

Formalities and Legalities

As soon as you are able, you will need to attend to certain formalities and legalities.

If friends or other family offer to assist you at this time, welcome their help. If the funeral has not been planned in advance, you will need to do so now, and, after your long sojourn at death's door, you probably will need assistance. The prime source of this assistance will be a funeral director, should you choose to hire one. If so, seek one with a good reputation for honesty and tact. Do not fall prey to unscrupulous funeral directors who try to profit from your family's grief. Ask your friends and family for recommendations.

Planning the Funeral

Nonprofit organizations also exist that will aid you in preparing the funeral. They can advise on the planning and help you in finding a competent funeral director who will not try to gain financially from your grief. If you are interested, call the Funeral Consumers Alliance at (800) 765-0107, or by visiting www.funerals.org on the Web. Try to find a local funeral home if at all possible, because the staff there will provide service at a more personal level than you will experience with a corporate-owned concern.

The fee for a funeral director should be several hundred dollars, though it can range into the thousands. A funeral director can help you with matters of flowers, donations to charity, and memorials, and assist in the composition of your loved one's obituary.

If you do not use a funeral director, reach out to siblings, other family, and friends to participate in the planning of the service. This event will be everyone's final farewell to your loved one, so try not to leave anybody out.

Decisions to Make, with Some Notes on Costs

Some preliminary decisions will have to be made:

- *Should the deceased be autopsied?* This is usually done if the cause of death is not known, but your physician may suggest that it be undertaken for research purposes. Your permission is needed to proceed on this course. Determine whether the procedure will leave the body in a state for viewing. The decision is yours, based on your own values, convictions, knowledge of your loved one, and your gut feelings.

- *Will the body be embalmed?* Bear in mind that nothing will prevent the body from decaying. Embalming serves a purpose, by delaying the process of decay, if the body needs to be moved some distance and remain presentable for a viewing. The practice originated during the American Civil War, when soldiers' bodies often had to travel a great distance before burial. Embalming costs between $200 and $500. Cosmetic preparation of the body for viewing starts at $50.

- *Will the body be interred, entombed, or cremated?* *Interment* is the most common course – the body is placed in a casket and buried in a cemetery. If it is *entombed,* the body will be placed a mausoleum, a building erected to house the caskets of the deceased of a family or other group. Caskets may be had for as little as $200 for a simple pine box. A cardboard box is also available, for around $20. Funeral homes are required by law to show you a list of all caskets available with descriptions and prices. Typically, relatives are shown three of the higher priced ones, and generally buy the one in the middle range. Ask to see the list, and ask if the list is complete.

  Finally, *cremation* reduces the remains to several pounds of ash and bone fragments. These are returned to the family, originally in an ordinary cardboard box. They may be moved to an urn (a procedure called *inurnment*), buried in the ground, placed in a mausoleum, or scattered. A viewing may precede a cremation, using a casket rented for about a third of what it costs. If no viewing is planned, you will need neither a casket nor embalming. The cost of cremation can be anywhere from around $100 to thousands, depending on how elaborate you want to become. Remember that, as more people opt for cremation of their remains, the funeral industry pioneers new ways to make money from it. Buy nothing but what you want.

- *What kind of service is appropriate?* It may be of any sort, whatever is most meaningful to your family. What would your loved one have wanted? Does the family want a joyful remembrance of a life well lived, or a religious reconciliation with death? It may even take on qualities of both. The service may be held in a church or synagogue, in a rented space, a public place, a garden, by the ocean, or even in a chapel at a funeral home, and it should not cost more than about $500. Wherever the service is held, remember that the keyword is "meaningful."

- *Is organ donation, or the body's bequeathing to science, a possibility?* If matters of organ donation arise, contact the Coalition on Donation at (804) 782-4920, or on the Web at www.shareyourlife.org. To explore the donation of the body to science, visit Biogift online at biogift.org, or by calling (866) 670-1799.

- *Is your loved one a veteran of the armed forces?* The Department of Veterans Affairs offers a number of benefits to former service members, including burial in a national cemetery with full military honors. The Department is on the Web at www.va.gov, and you may find your local office by clicking on "Locations" on the main page; or call (800) 827-1000.

- *Who will compose the obituary?* This document needs to be prepared with care, and with the understanding that the newspapers will rewrite it for purposes of space. As noted, a funeral director can assist here, should you employ one.

- *Will you need a vault or a grave liner?* These devices prevent the ground from sinking as the coffin crumbles over time. Depending on the material used, the cost can range from several hundred dollars to three or four times this much.

- *Is immediate burial or direct cremation an option?* These are package offerings that are simple and inexpensive. The body is buried or cremated immediately after death, and a memorial service is held at the later date, or if arranged, the same day as the funeral. These options should not exceed $1,000 in cost; be sure you know exactly what is included in the plan before you commit to it.

Legal Affairs

Certain *legal matters* will have to be addressed as well.

- You will need about a dozen copies of your parent's death certificate to attend to the final chores; you may get these from the mortuary, a funeral director, or the county clerk's office.

    Forward a copy of the certificate to Social Security and apply for the death benefit (about $250). Do the same with any other insurance policies, pensions, and retirement plans, as well as the Department of Veterans Affairs, if your parent served in the armed forces and is eligible for VA benefits.

- Find your parent's will and take it, along with the death certificate and file for probate – the legal process of validating a will as genuine - at your local court house or government center. You may omit this step on the advice of your attorney. Any deeds eventually will have to be changed; these are on file at your county registrar's office.

- Your parent's bank account will be frozen upon his death, and you will have no access to it, even if you have a power of attorney. I recommend that you open another account before your parent's passing, holding enough funds to pay for at least 6 months of bills. You will have immediate access to this account and with it, the ability to cover your loved one's previous commitments. Also inquire as to whether he had a safe deposit box. If so, and if it is not sealed by law upon his death, examine the contents.

- If his spouse remains alive, locate your parents' marriage license so she can file for benefits. You should be able to find this on file in the courthouse of the county in which they married.

- If dependent children remain alive, locate their birth certificates as well. These should be on file in the counties in which they were born.

- Notify all insurance companies of your parent's death. This includes health, life, mortgage, auto. accident, all credit cards, and any policies held by his employer. File any and all outstanding claims.

If your parent's spouse is alive, put the relevant policies into her name.

- Get in touch with your parent's former employers, who may owe pension benefits, salary, or back pay.
- List all assets and gather all titles and deeds. This list should include business partnerships or ownerships, stocks and bonds, savings and checking accounts, retirement accounts, pension plans, and profit-sharing plans. You will need to have the deeds of relevant properties transferred to their new owners.
- Locate your parent's last tax return. You will need to file one for the current year – the year in which he died.
- If your parent's spouse remains alive, you will need to revise her will to exclude the decedent from any inheritance.
- Notify any creditors of your parent's death, and begin the process of settling debts. Until the estate is closed, continue payment of any property taxes due.
- If your other parent is still alive, take all of these measures with her knowledge and permission. Never leave her out of any part of the process.

Again, this is a very time-consuming process, and highly emotional – you must repeat *my mother has died, my mother has died*, on phone call after phone call. And even though she is gone, just saying it over and over is heart wrenching. Also, bills in her name will continue to arrive for months. Just seeing my mother's name on letters and bills would put me into tears.

Settling the Estate

You will eventually have to undertake the division of your deceased parent's estate. Wills usually indicate that these properties should be divided equally, but beyond the money in the estate, the equality of property may be a sticking point. Keepsakes and mementos are examples of priceless items of inheritance.

Ideally, you will wait for some weeks or a month before settling the estate, to let emotions level off. Assign values to items the worth of which can be estimated in dollars; then apportion the inheritance by these dollar amounts.

For items that are beyond any monetary value, ask each family member to list those things he or she most values, and try to distribute these items fairly. If necessary, ask a third party – a friend of the family respected by all – to mediate the process. You might want to plan to take several breaks during this apportioning process, particularly if there are many such priceless mementos and photographs.

Grief

Of course, while you address all these points of social custom and legal requirement, you also, along with all your siblings and other relatives, grieve the passing of your parent. And in the matter of grief, we are in the realm of the incommensurable.

Every family member will experience in some way all of the emotions and reactions identified by Elizabeth Kübler-Ross and discussed earlier. The initial response of the primary caregiver is likely to be stunned disbelief, coupled, perhaps, with an element of relief that her parent's long journey to the end is finally over.

None of these feelings, emotions, thoughts, or reactions should be judged. All should be experienced, endured, explored, and let go.

You and your siblings may discover yourselves angry with your parent for abandoning you, or you may feel guilty about things said and done, and left unsaid and undone. You may resent others whose parents are still alive. You may even have issues now surfacing with your brothers and sisters. These are all natural feelings. Just take a breath and deal with them one day at a time.

Physical Effects of Grieving

The death may have physical effects as well, as grief weakens your immune system, upsets your hormonal balance, alters your appetite, and disrupts sleeping patterns. Everyone in the family needs to learn to ask for help with their feelings of loss, from family, friends, and coworkers. Stoicism may seem noble, but it is worse than useless and functions much like denial, with similar consequences, prolonging your suffering. Do not try to manage your grief, to respond to it as you feel you "should." There is no timeline to follow. You recover when you recover, not a minute before, and not "too late." You grieve as long as you must. *You go through everything right on time.*

Children, Death, and Grieving

And this is true for all members of your family, including any children. Children, even very young children, are affected by the process of dying, death, and grief, often in ways they cannot articulate. At the outset of the caregiving project, talk honestly with your children about what is happening.

Children take adults' words literally, so you should avoid language like *God took Grandma away* or *She went to sleep and will never wake again.* Explain that in old age our bodies cease to work as they have all our lives, and so we pass away.

Assure the children that the deceased is not in any pain, and characterize death as the natural end of life, not a punishment or a state of suffering.

And After . . .

Life does go on: grief becomes experience. If your late parent was the sole surviving one, you may discover a new sense of who you are and what you want – a different kind of independence, now that your parents are gone, accompanied by a renewed value of self. This understanding can help you to find different goals for your energies and intelligence, now free of the duties of a caregiver. There is no doubt that because of this experience you will become a different person. The question is, who will that person be?

Regarding the Surviving Spouse

If your other parent still lives, she (or he) will need your continued attention and support. You will have to deal with your own grief, of course, but you will want to remain in touch with your surviving parent, and will probably devote a good bit of your time to helping her deal with loss. Help her to remain in touch with the rest of her world – to get out and about, to see old friends, make new ones, and perhaps do things that her previous life kept her from doing. You undoubtedly will now become her caregiver, and the cycle continues.

Be especially attentive around holidays, and especially in the first year following her spouse's death. Private holidays, wedding anniversaries and birthdays, can be even more important than public ones. It is usually the "firsts" that impact everyone the most – the first Father's Day, the first birthday, the first Easter. It is also the first time you start to call your loved one and realize that she will not answer.

Just as the death of a parent can bring about unexpected changes in your life, so can it in the life of your surviving parent. You may witness surprising changes in her new life as a single person, in positive or unusual ways or in sadness. Everyone reacts differently. Don't be surprised if your surviving parent begins to date again!

Your surviving parent will want to avoid big decisions until her grief has passed a bit. In the meantime, she should take care of herself, and that included grief counseling, if she feels it is necessary. AARP offers such a service, called the Grief and Loss Program; contact AARP at (888) 687-2277, or on the Web at www.aarp.org.

CHAPTER 13

After it all . . .

Your loved one has now passed on. All the final arrangements and legal issues have been resolved. You are now left alone with your thoughts. You might have feelings of relief, or exhaustion, of even disbelief that it is really all over. You might even feel numb, sad, or empty. You may be a bit lost, wondering what you are supposed to do next. Your life has been totally consumed with your "job" as a senior caregiver that you might be wondering how you will now fill your time. The phone was always ringing for you, you were always worried, and you seemed to be constantly distracted, you were juggling all the balls in the air; you were the "go to" person. You were making decisions moment to moment, you felt guilty, and yet you were feeling that at least you were "doing something." But what, exactly? It's not like you were caregiving a baby, where you were seeing delightful positive progress every day or week, or getting such a burst of excitement at one's first steps, or the loss of a tooth, or first words. No, you were just helping someone to die. You were watching and directly involved with the final phase of someone's life, the transition. Nothing about this time was really happy, but I think the only word that comes to mind is meaningful. In my dad's final moments I said to him, "You were here for my first breath, and I am here for your last". It was a very profound time to realize the clock had stopped ticking and there will be no more.

You will be forever changed once a senior caregiver. You will look at life differently. Your family and friends will take on new meaning, and love will grow deeper or may just disappear. Life will become of new value to you. But, one thing for sure is that your heart can be nothing but full and your soul lifted.

RESOURCES

Books

Jane Gross, *Bittersweet Season: Caring for Our Aging Parents – and Ourselves*

Elizabeth Kubler-Ross, *On Death and Dying*

C. S. Lewis, *A Grief Observed*

Mary Pipher, Ph.D., *Another Country: Navigating the Emotional Terrain of Our Elders*

Internet

Commission on Accreditation of Rehabilitation Facilities
Carf.org

Elder Locator
"a public service of the U.S. Administration on Aging connecting you to services for older adults and their families"
1-800-677-1116
www.eldercare.gov/Eldercare.NET/Public/Index.aspx

HIPAA
www.hhs.gov/ocr/privacy/hipaa/understanding/summary/index.html

Joint Commission on the Accreditation of Healthcare Organizations
www.Jointcommission.org

Medicare – the official government website
www.Medicare.gov/default.aspx
www.medicare.gov/MedicareEligibility/home.asp

Medicare.org – a non-government resource
(888) 815-3313
www.medicare.org

National Assn of Area Agencies on Aging
www.n4a.org

National Assn of Professional Geriatric Care Managers
(602) 881-8008
www.caremanager.org

Nursing Home Compare
www.medicare.gov/NHCompare